Foreword

CIRIA's environmental research programme includes the provision of guidance for construction and waste professionals in relation to the minimisation, reuse and recycling of construction wastes and surplus materials. Ground engineering works give rise to very large volumes of excavated spoil, increasingly so as more works such as roads and railways are built in cutting and tunnel. This report provides guidance for good practice in managing spoil from ground works through planning, design and construction. It is the outcome of CIRIA Research Project 544: *Disposal of ground engineering waste: a review study.*

Section 2 of the report was written under contract to CIRIA by Dr J S Sceal and Miss F E Bryson of Wardell Armstrong and Section 3 by Mr J Bickerdike and Ms J Stanbury of Scott Wilson Kirkpatrick & Co. Ltd. The survey and case studies were made by Miss J C T Kwan of CIRIA who with Mr F M Jardine, also of CIRIA, prepared the report. As is normal CIRIA practice the research was guided by a steering group which comprised.

Mr S Clamp (Chairman)	–	Gibb Ltd
Mr J Bickerdike	–	Scott Wilson Kirkpatrick & Co Ltd
Mr D Bliss	–	The Environment Agency
Mr N J Bradbury	–	Kvaerner Cementation Foundations
Mr P Crowcroft	–	Aspinwall and Company
Dr A Fawcett	–	Keller Ground Engineering
Mr M Hassall	–	Wardell Armstrong
Mr M Haynes	–	Thorburn Colquhoun
Dr A K Hughes	–	Rofe Kennard & Lapworth
Mr D R V Jones	–	Golder Associates (UK) Ltd
Ms J Luckhurst	–	North West Water Ltd
Mr A Phear	–	Rail Link Engineering
Mr C R Pugh	–	C A Blackwell (Contracts) Ltd
Mr M P Pugh	–	Binnie Black & Veatch
Mr J Moriarty	–	London Underground Ltd
Dr N J O'Riordan	–	Rail Link Engineering
Mr G Muir	–	Alfred McAlpine Construction Ltd
Mr C D T Wood	–	Henry Boot Construction (UK) Ltd
Mr C Worthing	–	Wimtec Environmental Ltd

CIRIA's Research Managers for this project were Mr F M Jardine and Miss J C T Kwan.

The project was funded by:

Construction Sponsorship Directorate of the Department of the Environment, Transport and the Regions (formerly known as the Department of the Environment) C A Blackwell (Contracts) Ltd

CIRIA is grateful for the help, information and illustrative material given not only by the funders and the members of the Steering Group, but also by the clients, engineers and contractors of projects involved in the questionnaire survey and the case studies. In alphabetical order, they are:

Terry Adams Ltd
John Allen Associates
AMEC Civil Engineering Limited
Amey Construction Limited
Ove Arup & Partners
Aspinwall & Company
WS Atkins Consultants Limited
Balfour Beatty Tilbury-Douglas Asphalt
Ballast Wiltshire Plc
Bechtel Water Technology
Birse Construction Limited
Henry Boot Construction (UK) Ltd
British Gas
British Waterways
Canary Wharf Ltd
Cheetham Hill Construction Limited
Connect A50 Limited
Costain Civil Engineering Ltd
Derby Pride Limited
Derbyshire County Council
Fox Contracting (Owmby) Limted
GEC Alsthom Power Generation
Golder Associates (UK) Ltd
Greenbank St Helens Limited
Halliburton Brown & Root Ltd
Highways Agency
Hyder Consulting Limited
Keller Ground Engineering
Kvaerner Cementation Foundations

Land Securities Plc
Landfill Management Limited
Leicester City Challenge Ltd
London Underground Limited
Alfred McAlpine Civil Engineering
Alfred McAlpine Construction Ltd
McNicholas Construction Co Ltd
Mott MacDonald Group
National Power
North West Water Ltd
Edmund Nuttall Limited
Pearson Whitfield
Rail Link Engineering
J Sainsbury Plc
Scott Wilson Kirkpatrick & Co. Ltd
Stent Foundations Limited
Stirling Maynard and Partners
Tarmac – Bachy Joint Venture
Tarmac Construction
The MSL Consultancy
Thorburn Colquhoun
Wallis Western
Wardell Armstrong
White Cliffs Countryside Project
Wimpey – Amey Joint Venture
Wolverhampton Metropolitan Borough Council

NL
S/O:

Report 179   1997

UNIVERSITY OF STRATHCLYDE

30125 00561399 6

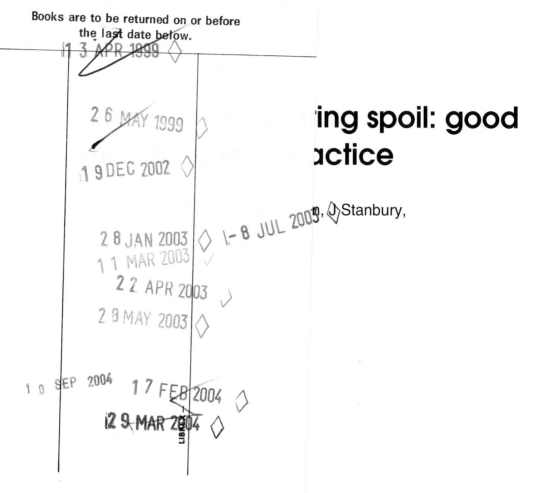

ing spoil: good
actice

Stanbury,

CONSTRUCTION INDUSTRY RESEARCH AND INFORMATION ASSOCIATION
6 Storey's Gate, Westminster, SW1 P 3AU
Tel: 0171 222 8891   Fax: 0171 222 1708
E-mail: switchboard@ciria.org.uk

STRATHCLYDE

Summary

A large proportion of the waste generated in UK is surplus spoil arising from excavation on construction sites. This report is a result of a research study about design and construction practice in the management of spoil. The research includes a survey of 40 recent construction projects, detailed case study of six of those and reviews of both the legal requirements for the disposal of spoil and of current and emerging practices in the recycling or reuse and minimisation of surplus spoil with the introduction of the landfill tax in October 1996, the conclusions drawn from the research and the recommendations for practice provide important lessons for planners, construction clients, designers and contractors.

The main lessons are: (1) that the management of spoil requires care throughout a construction project, particularly in regard to the time to obtain relevant permissions and for complying with legislation; (2) that careful spoil management can result in financial benefit to clients and contractors; (3) that two important steps are early and regular consultation with the regulatory authorities; and (4) that spoil management should be included in the project brief from the start.

J C T Kwan, J S Sceal, F E Bryson, J Stanbury, J Bickerdike and F M Jardine
Ground engineering spoil: good management practice
Construction Industry Research and Information Association
CIRIA Report 179, 1997

© CIRIA 1997

ISBN: 0 86017 484 0

ISSN: 0 305 408 X

Keywords		
Waste disposal, ground engineering, earthworks, spoil recycling, reuse, waste minimisation		
Reader Interest	**Classification**	
Construction, geotechnical and environmental engineers, planners, waste management professionals, local authorities	AVAILABILITY	Restricted
	CONTENT	Guidance practice case study and survey of current practices
	STATUS	Committee guided
	USER	Construction and waste management professionals, planners

CONTENTS

List of figures

List of tables

GLOSSARY

difficult waste　　Waste which is difficult to handle because of its chemical, biochemical or physical properties

disposal　　Operations by which a material is removed from its source and deposited elsewhere temporarily or permanently

recycling　　One of the waste recovery operation which involves processing the waste to produce a useable raw material, e.g. lime stabilisation of a soft soil

reduction　　Reducing the amount of waste produced

reuse　　Where material is designed to be used again in more or less its original condition or where discarded products are found new uses with minimal processing

special waste　　Waste materials exhibiting specified, hazardous properties, as defined in the Special Waste Regulations 1996 which also provide a schedule of substances that are classified as special wastes

spoil　　Soil or rock or other earth material arising from excavation, dredging, or other ground engineering work

surplus spoil　　Spoil that is extra to the requirements of the construction project's permanent works design

unsuitable spoil　　Spoil which is not suitable for use in permanent works because of its properties

waste　　(from DoE Circular 11/94; the Regulations referred to are the Waste Management Licensing Regulations 1994) The Definition of Waste : Basic Principles

In order for a substance or object to be waste it must:

- fall into one of the categories (substances or objects which are waste when discarded) set out in Part II of Schedule 4 to the Regulations **and**:

- be discarded, disposed of or got rid of by the holder: or

- be intended to be discarded, disposed of or got rid of by the holder; or

- be required to be discarded, disposed of or got rid of by the holder.

waste minimisation　　Any technique, process or activity which either avoids, eliminates or reduces waste at its source or allows reuse or recycling of the waste for benign purposes.

Abbrevations

CIRIA	Construction Industry Research Information and Association
COTC	Certificate of Technical Competence
DBFO	Design/build/finance/operate
DCPs	Development Control Policy Notes
DoE	Department of the Environment
DOT	Department of Transport
EA	Environment Agency
EC	European Commission
HA	Highways Commission
HMSO	Her Majesty's Stationery Office (now known as The Stationery Office)
HSE	Health & Safety Executive
ICRCL	Interdepartmental Committee on the Reclamation of Contaminated Land
MPGs	Mineral Planning Guidance Notes
NA	Not available
NCPGs	National Control Policy Guidance Notes (Scotland)
OECD	Organisation for Economic Cooperation and Development
PAH	Polynuclear aromatic hydrocarbon
PCB	Polychlorinated biphenol
PFA	Pulverised fuel ash
PPGs	Planning Policy Guidance Notes
RPGs	Regional Planning Guidance Notes
SEPA	Scottish Environmental Protection Agency
SPGs	Strategic Planning Guidance Notes
TBM	Tunnel Boring Machine
UDP	Unitary Development Plan
WMP	Waste Management Paper

1   Introduction

1.1   BACKGROUND

Construction operations produce large volumes of surplus excavated materials. The waste from construction and demolition works is thought to total about 25 million tonnes per year but increasing to over 70 million tonnes when surplus excavated material is included. Much of this material is soil and rock excavated for new roads, tunnels and foundations to structures. Furthermore, the lack of suitable (and close) landfill sites has significantly increased disposal costs on some projects in recent years, the works for London Underground's Jubilee Line Extension being a particular example, involving very large volumes of spoil from tunnel and station excavations. Disposal costs have further increased with the introduction of the weight-based landfill tax in October 1996. They are expected to continue to rise as a result of government policy to use the tax as a means of reducing the amount of waste sent to landfill.

There is both increasing pressure and incentive, therefore, to minimise the amount of construction spoil sent to landfill sites, but to do so depends on being able to reduce, recycle and reuse more of it. That, in turn, calls for reliable information about how construction sites handle wastes, and spoil from ground engineering operations in particular. Reduction, reuse or recycling of spoil will only be a viable option if considered as such in the design, operation and management of the works taken as a whole and not as separate activities, i.e. planned in relation to the construction project, its locality and its timing, and in detail at operator level for individual tasks. As a step towards gaining the type of information to help that planning, this CIRIA research project considers a range of different construction projects and the way they are dealing with different types of spoil or arisings from ground engineering operations.

For simplicity, the term 'spoil' as used in the rest of this report refers to soil, rock or other ground materials which are excavated (e.g. the material taken to form a cutting, or arisings from a trench or foundation excavation or tunnel, and which may be temporarily stockpiled). In some cases the spoil will be a mixture of ground materials with the products used in certain geotechnical processes (e.g. bentonite slurry, grout).

Use of the term, spoil, which is familiar to civil and geotechnical engineers, therefore, does not have the connotation of something being damaged, but as something 'won' from the ground. As such the term is intended to be neutral, there being no presumption either of automatic reuse (as, for example, cut-and-fill earthworks would suggest) or of disposal as waste. Surplus spoil is not necessarily 'unsuitable' material as, for a different use, it might well be suitable. Surplus spoil, therefore, is the material from the ground not needed to complete the project which generates it.

This report presents the results of: (1) a survey of 40 projects, seeking the views of clients, consulting engineers and contractors, (2) more detailed case study by interview of principal staff concerned with six projects, and (3) general reviews of relevant legislation and current practice.

This report is for CIRIA's members and other construction professionals, particularly clients, their designers and contractors. The lessons apply to most construction sites, all of which start with groundworks.

These lessons for practice can be summarised as:

- identification of the key elements of, and main problems in, current practice in relation to spoil from ground engineering operations
- examples of possible solutions for these problems
- a description of the influence of legislation relating to waste disposal on current and emerging construction practice
- guidance as to what is considered to be good practice in managing different forms and types of spoil
- improvements to the planning, design and construction operations that would make for better management of spoil in terms of cost-efficiency and higher environmental standards
- ways in which ground engineering works can apply waste minimisation, reuse and recycling effectively.

1.2   RESEARCH METHODS

There were two main information-gathering stages in this project. They were:

1. By questionnaire survey. The survey examined how different types and forms of spoil generated from ground engineering operations are reused, recycled, or disposed as waste. Separate questionnaires were designed for clients, consulting engineers and contractors. In addition to gathering indicative numerical data (on quantities, costs, etc.) the questionnaires asked about:

- priorities in relation to spoil in the design and implementation of projects
- effects of legal requirements on spoil management
- consent requirements of the planning authorities, the Environment Agency and other regulatory bodies.

The survey covered 40 projects involving more than twenty different types of ground engineering operations. The projects were offered to CIRIA for study, rather than being chosen at random, and are therefore not necessarily representative of the whole industry. Section 4 of this report presents and discusses the results of the survey.

2. By case studies. Six construction projects were studied in detail, with the following objectives:

- to identify the disposal routes or reuse options, chosen for the surplus spoil of the project
- to identify the criteria used by different parties involved in the disposal as waste, or the reuse and recycling of spoil
- to examine how different stages of a project affected the disposal, reuse and recycling of spoil
- to draw out lessons of general application to the management of spoil in practice.

In each case study, in addition to the information provided on the replies to the questionnaires, CIRIA staff interviewed key personnel of the project. Section 5 of the report presents the findings of the case studies.

The information about the projects was given to CIRIA staff in confidence on the understanding that neither the projects, the persons involved nor the organisations would be identified in any use of the information or subsequent report on the research.

The report maintains that requirement for anonymity, referring only to projects by code number.

1.3   LIMITATIONS AND DIFFICULTIES

The information gained from the research depended heavily on the return rate of the questionnaires and the responses at the interviews. The return rate was 53% being 64 responses out of a possible 120 and relating to 32 of the 40 projects targetted, i.e. 80%. Although this return rate was good, there were a number of difficulties for the research. These were:

1. The selective approach of the questionnaire survey means that it does not neccessary yield a complete picture of national practice.

2. The sample size is too small to provide statistically reliable data.

3. The projects were diverse and over a wide geographical area.

4. The amount of information and level of detail that the participants of the case studies and the questionnaire were able to provide varied.

Limitations of resource and time restricted the research to only a small number of case studies, and the results may not represent the views of the construction industry as a whole.

1.4   OUTLINE OF THE REPORT

This project report comprises six sections.

Section 2 is a summary of the legal requirements of waste disposal relevant to ground engineering spoil. As well as considering the influence of UK and EU regulations and policy on disposal, reuse and recycling of spoil, it also provides introductory guidance about interpretation of the legislation.

Section 3 presents and examines a range of options used in current practice for managing ground engineering spoil. In this section there is particular emphasis on:

- consideration, in the planning design and construction stages, of the potential problems of surplus spoil and its becoming a waste

- the roles of client, designer and contractor

- methods for reducing, reusing and recycling spoil, thereby minimising waste.

Section 4, supported by data in Appendix 1, is a summary of the results of the questionnaire survey. It considers some aspects of practice, generally on fairly large projects, prior to introduction of the landfill tax in October 1996. This section includes commentary on data quality and presentation. The small number and diversity of projects surveyed meant that it was not possible to draw general conditions from the data.

The case study reports are in Section 5. The description of each case-study project follows a standard format, although not all in the same degree of detail. Rather, the aim is to present only such information as is needed to support the particular lesson drawn from the project.

The final section (6) of the report presents conclusions drawn from the study and puts forward recommendations about the management of spoil from ground engineering operations for the planning, design and construction stages of projects.

2   Legal requirements

In recent years the evolution of environmental law, and waste management law in particular, has been fast and keeping pace with these changes has been a challenge to the industry and administrators alike. It is less than twenty five years since statutory requirements i.e., the Deposit of Poisonous Wastes Act 1972 and the Control of Pollution Act, 1974, were introduced specifically to control wastes and the operation of disposal sites. Since then a plethora of legislation and guidance has issued from the European Union, central government and its agencies.

In addition, attitudes toward waste have undergone considerable change during this period, notably towards waste minimisation and sustainable waste management practices. This has culminated in the recent Department of Environment publication *Making Waste Work*[1] which sets out the government's strategy for achieving more sustainable waste management and engendering responsible attitudes towards waste generation and management. The message from the document is: '*more sustainable waste practices need not entail great expense or restrictive legislation. Indeed they can bring substantial savings to business*'.

A sound understanding of the regulatory framework controlling waste management activities is an important component in the management of ground engineering projects. These, almost without exception, give rise to surplus materials which, if no use can be found for them, become classified as wastes.

An appreciation of the time-scales involved, in following the various regulatory routes, is important. In particular, clients need to be aware that protracted negotiations with the regulators during the application of various consents for the project (including those needed for reuse, recycling and disposal of spoil) are not uncommon and should be taken account of in framing project deadlines. Early consideration should be given to the project's spoil management requirements and pre-emptive discussions with the authorities should be considered.

The increasing climate in favour of sustainable waste management practices is likely to encourage waste minimisation, reuse, and recovery of spoil, particularly where this is accompanied by tangible financial benefits.

This section reviews the range of regulatory controls over waste management practices and introduces and describes the concept of sustainable waste management. Special care should be taken in the interpretation of legal documents and the following review comprises only an outline. Relevant legal or experienced advice should be sought from the Environment Agency in cases where the situation or application of the legal framework is not clear cut.

Note that this section does not cover other requirements of the law, such as health and safety regulations, e.g. COSHH.

2.1   SUSTAINABLE WASTE MANAGEMENT

Sustainable waste management, as set out in the DoE's strategy document, is a fundamental part of the Government's commitment to sustainable development [2]. The key message is that more sustainable waste management is a realistic goal and one which can be attained without excessive expense or regulation and, moreover, it can bring with it significant economic savings.

In order to prioritise waste management activities a waste hierarchy has been formulated as follows:

- waste minimisation
- reuse of waste
- waste recovery
- waste disposal.

The waste hierarchy identifies waste minimisation as the most sustainable of the waste management options. In terms of ground engineering, this would be applicable, for example, to making sure that there is a cut-and-fill balance in appropriate civil engineering projects and that the method of storage of raw materials prevents or reduces wastage as far as possible. Further information and guidance on waste reduction in construction projects is available in a recent CIRIA publication [3, 44-46].

The **reuse** of waste has a specific meaning and is distinct from recycling. Reuse is defined as either where products are used again in more or less their original condition or where discarded products are found new uses with minimal processing.

Waste **recovery** includes **recycling** and processing of the waste to produce a useable material. Waste recovery is placed lower down the waste hierarchy because of the necessary energy and processing costs associated with it. Recycling is commonly used in ground engineering projects, e.g., concrete and other building materials crushed for use as fill, blacktop planings, etc.

Waste **disposal** comes at the bottom of the waste hierarchy and as such is the least favoured option for sustainable waste management. Waste disposal largely comprises final disposal to landfill and incineration without energy recovery. In practice, waste disposal accounts for about 70% of all controlled wastes; they are mainly sent to landfill.

DoE statistics indicate that up to 70 million tonnes of construction and demolition wastes (which includes spoil) are generated annually in UK and that, of this, 30% is recovered, usually as bulk fill and 63% goes to landfill [4].

2.2 THE REGULATORY FRAMEWORK

2.2.1 The influence of the European Union

The regulatory framework within which all waste management activities must operate has, to a great extent, been completely revised during the 1990s and continues to be in a state of change. This section sets out the current (1997) regulatory framework for the management of waste and describes the regulatory conditions which are likely to be encountered by those dealing with ground engineering projects.

As in all other fields, the influence of the European Union is strong in UK waste management legislation and all waste recovery or waste disposal operations must comply with the *Framework Directive on Waste* [5]. This directive establishes a set of rules by which waste management procedures are to be formalised and standardised throughout the European Union. Various other EC Directives have also had an effect on the UK waste management framework, the most important of which are the Directives dealing with hazardous wastes [6] and groundwater protection [7].

Long-running attempts to standardise the European landfill industry, however, have so far failed, with the withdrawal of the Directive *Landfilling of Waste* [8]. A revised proposal for a EU Council *Directives on landfill of waste* was issued in March 1997 by the European Commission. This had not been adopted by the EU when this report was prepared (i.e July 1997).

Member countries are clearly in a position to implement and operate other complementary national legislation but must, as a minimum, comply with the appropriate EC Directive. This is most apparent in the UK's national planning regime, which incorporates the requirements of the Environmental Impact Assessment Directive [9], into a system which was established during the 1940s.

2.2.2   Regulating Authorities

Regulation of waste management activities in the UK falls within the remit of a variety of organisations. In England and Wales, the waste planning regime falls largely within the remit of the county councils and, in metropolitan areas, district councils. In Scotland, the waste management planning regime falls within the remit of the Regional Councils.

In general terms, all waste management activities must be in possession of an appropriate planning permission from one of the above authorities before they can proceed to the second 'permitting' stage. This second stage, which generally comprises an application for a waste management licence, is regulated in England and Wales by the Environment Agency (EA), and in Scotland by the Scottish Environmental Protection Agency (SEPA).

In addition, district councils in England, Wales and Scotland are vested with specific environmental protection powers. These cover 'nuisance' controls [10] and local authority air pollution control powers [11]. The Environment Agency and SEPA also have a wide variety of powers to protect controlled waters [12] inherited from the former National Rivers Authority and River Purification Boards.

2.2.3   Definition of waste

The definition of waste, and the process by which materials are determined to be or not to be waste, has always been very problematic. However, guidance in DoE circular 11/94 [13] relating to England, Wales and Scotland has clarified the situation somewhat and has transposed the requirements of the *Framework Directive on Waste* [5] to UK legislation.

Fundamentally, the status of a material as a waste is considered from the viewpoint of the current holder of the material (defined in DoE Circular 11/94 as the producer or the person in possession of a substance or object [13]), and it is the responsibility of the holder to decide whether the material is waste, and if so, to take the necessary actions in relation to the material.

A central feature of the definition of waste, as set out in paragraph 2-18, Annex 2 of Circular 11/94 [13], is the concept of discarding, intending to discard or being required to discard substances or objects. Paragraph 2.18 is as follows:

> *The Definition of Waste : Basic Principles*
>
> *In order for a substance or object to be waste it must:*
>
> - *fall into one of the categories (substances or objects which are waste when discarded) set out in Part II of Schedule 4 to the Regulations **and**:*
>   - *be discarded, disposed of or got rid of by the holder; or*
>   - *be intended to be discarded, disposed of or got rid of by the holder; or*
>   - *be required to be discarded, disposed of or got rid of by the holder.*
>
> (The Regulations referred to are the Waste Management Licensing Regulations 1994 [14])

It should be stressed that the system for the classification of waste remains to be proven, and that its strict interpretation is a matter for the Courts. There is as yet very little UK case law on the definition of waste. Therefore any advice offered would be largely speculative.

All waste, which becomes classified under the terms of the Waste Framework Directive, is termed 'Directive Waste'. (The term commonly used in the UK until recently was 'controlled waste'. Technically almost all controlled waste should now be known as Directive Waste.)

In the past, wastes have been categorised according to various physical, chemical or biological properties. There are currently moves to harmonise the existing classification systems in the form of international and national Waste Lists, of which several are developed, or about to be developed. These include the following:

- OECD Waste List (which has been implemented into EC legislation) [15] and is used largely for the import and export of wastes between OECD and non-OECD countries

- European Waste Catalogue [16]

- European Hazardous Waste List (now implemented into UK legislation via the Special Waste Regulations 1996) [17]

- UK Waste Classification List (currently in draft)[18]. This is being produced largely to assist in waste management planning, but may also be used for regulatory purposes.

2.3   WASTE MANAGEMENT PLANNING

The planning system controls the development and use of land in the public interest. The UK planning control system underwent a major overhaul in the early 1990s, at which time a set of consolidating statutes were introduced in order to simplify the previous system. The current primary legislation directing the planning system includes:

- Town and Country Planning Act 1990

- Planning and Compensation Act 1991.

The planning control system is briefly reviewed below, initially to provide an overview of the legislative and executive planning framework and then to reference specific controls applicable to waste management activities. The system is divided into three main categories as follows:

- Planning and policy guidance

- The development plan

- Development control.

2.3.1 Planning and policy guidance

In addition to primary legislation, the UK government publishes numerous other statements of planning policy and guidance which play an important role in the planning control system. Such policy statements and guidance may be found in:

- Planning circulars
- White Papers
- Ministerial Statements
- Planning Policy Guidance Notes (PPGs)
- Minerals Planning Guidance Notes (MPGs)
- Strategic Planning Guidance Notes (SPGs)
- Regional Planning Guidance Notes (RPGs)
- Development Control Policy Notes (DCPs)
- National Control Policy Guidance Notes (NCPGs) (Scotland).

PPGs, MPGs and RPGs are the principal source of policy guidance on planning issues in England and Wales, while planning circulars focus more on legislative and procedural matters. All these documents are available from HMSO.

There is currently no specific planning guidance document relating to waste and this gap has been acknowledged by the Department of the Environment (DoE) (particularly in consideration of the wide range of guidance, in the form of MPGs for the minerals industry). In order to redress this balance the DoE has proposed to revise the current general planning guidance on pollution control [19] to include specific guidance on waste management planning. At the time of writing, the proposed revision has been produced as a draft for public consultation (dated September 1996).

2.3.2 The development plan

The development plan system is an important part of the planning control system and generally provides a 'first stop' reference source for proposed development. The development plan system is administered largely on a two-tier basis; first at county council level and then at district council area. Exceptions to this are unitary authorities (i.e. the metropolitan district councils of Greater London and Greater Manchester, and the new unitary authorities introduced under local government reorganisation in 1996), where both tiers are administered by the same authority. Other exceptions include the National Parks which are indepedent planning authorities.

The first tier of the development plan system comprises the Structure Plan [20], which is defined as *'a written statement formulating the local planning authority's policy and general proposals in respect of development and other use of land in their area'*. The Structure Plan is thus primarily a written statement of policies and is usually illustrated with a key diagram. Its function is to describe broad policy, but not to provide details of specific land uses.

The second tier of the development plan system comprises a range of Local Plans. There are two main types of local plans (a less common type is the Action Area Plan), as follows:

- 'True' local plans, which expand information contained in the relevant structure plan by providing geographically specific details of approved development uses, proposed roads and other land uses, green belt zones, environmentally sensitive areas, etc.
- Subject local plans, which expand structure plan information in relation to specialised development types, e.g. minerals local plan.

Structure, local plans and waste management plans have to be compatible with central government policies, and represent the primary documents to which the developer and the planning authorities should refer for guidance in relation to new development proposals.

Development plans in metropolitan and unitary authorities comprise Unitary Development Plans (UDPs) Parts 1 and 2 which are equivalent to the structure and local plan system of the shire counties.

The concept of a 'plan-led system' was introduced by the Planning and Compensation Act 1991, where structure plans and local plans are given considerable importance in the determination of planning applications. It is stated that [21] *'Where, in making any determination under the planning Acts, regard is to be had to the development plan, the determination shall be made in accordance with the plan unless material considerations indicate otherwise'*. A planning authority may not go against its structure or local plan without stating clearly what *'material considerations'* have been taken into account.

2.3.3   Development control

In the majority of cases it is necessary for a formal application for planning permission to be made and granted before any development can take place. Certain exceptions to this are prescribed [22] or permitted [23] developments, but these are not generally applicable to waste management activities, as they relate to minor developments or minor changes to existing developments.

Application for planning permission is normally made by the completion of a form obtained from the planning authority and the payment of an application fee. In many cases, the information contained in the form will usually be supplemented by further documentation including, in specific cases, information relating to potential environmental impacts. This is described in the following paragraphs.

Certain categories of development fall within the requirements of the Town and Country Planning (Assessment of Environmental Effects) Regulations 1988. These categories are generally those which are most likely to give rise to significant environmental impacts.

The 1988 Regulations describe the requirements of the environmental assessment process which is defined as follows:

> *a technique and a process by which information about the environmental effects of a project is collected, both by the developer and from other sources, and taken into account by the planning authority in forming their judgement on whether the development should go ahead.*

The undertaking of an environmental assessment (documented in an environmental statement) in support of a planning application is compulsory for certain prescribed categories of development (referred to as 'Schedule 1 projects') and is optional for other prescribed categories (referred to as 'Schedule 2 projects').

Following the submission of the planning application and supporting documentation it is considered by the planning authority in relation to published policy (see Structure and Local plans above) and consultations with various statutory and non-statutory bodies, and including the Environment Agency. Government guidance [24] states that:

> *The planning system .... should operate on the basis that applications for development should be allowed, having regard to the development plan and all material considerations, unless the proposed development would cause demonstrable harm to interests of acknowledged importance.*

The determination of planning applications should, strictly speaking, be made within eight weeks of the application date. On certain projects where an Environmental Statement is submitted in support of an application, determinations should be made within sixteen weeks. Allowance is made in the relevant legislation [25] for this period to be extended with the agreement of both planning authority and the applicant.

Where planning permission is given, this is normally subject to a series of conditions which regulate the development or use of any land under the control of the applicant. The planning authority is however constrained from indiscriminate imposition of conditions (see DoE Circular 1/85) [26].

In addition to planning conditions, the planning authority and the developers (or land owners) may enter into certain planning agreements [27] or planning obligations [28].

Finally, when planning applications are refused or conditions, unacceptable to the developer, are imposed the applicant has the right of appeal to the Secretary of State for the Environment.

2.4   WASTE MANAGEMENT LICENSING IN ENGLAND AND WALES

In England and Wales a Waste Management Licence is normally required (in addition to relevant planning permission) for waste management facilities. Whereas the planning regime controls the use of land, the licensing system, administered by the Environment Agency, is intended to control activities at a facility and any licence issued will be subject to conditions which are considered necessary to prevent:

- pollution of the environment
- harm to human health
- serious detriment to the amenities of the locality.

The terms of reference of the Environment Agency with respect to waste management licensing are set out in The Waste Management Licensing Regulations 1994 [14,29] (as amended). These regulations define three types of waste management activities, as follows;

- activities which require licensing
- activities for which exemption from the licensing regime can be applied
- activities which are excluded from licensing, as they are regulated by other control regimes.

The application and regulatory requirements for each of the three types of waste management activities above are discussed in the following sections. The disposal of ground engineering wastes could fall into any of the above categories, but most likely into one of the first two.

The Waste Management Licence is held by the operator. There are provisions within the Environmental Protection Act 1990 to transfer licences (Section 40 of the Act) and the licence holder and the proposed transferee should jointly make an application to the Environment Agency. The transferee is required to meet the various licence requirements including the fit-and-proper person provisions. The site remains the responsibility of the licence holder who will maintain a monitoring regime and pay the required subsistence fees until a certificate of completion is issued by the Agency.

2.4.1 Licensable activities

A waste management licence, as defined in Section 35(1) of the Environmental Protection Act 1990, is required for *'the treatment, keeping or disposal of any specific description of controlled waste (see Section 2.2) in or on specified land or the treatment or disposal of any specified description of controlled waste by means of specified mobile plant'*.

In practice, those involved in waste management activities should be prepared to put a case to the Environment Agency as to why the activity should be exempt or excluded from the licensing system. If the activity is not specifically exempt or excluded, waste management licensing will normally be necessary.

Waste management licensing places a significant financial and management obligation on those undertaking the activity. This obligation continues during the time of the activity and extends until such a time as the land on which the activity has been undertaken, e.g. the landfill, is determined (by the Environment Agency) to be *'unlikely to cause pollution of the environment or harm to human health'* [30]. At this stage the licence can be 'surrendered' (on application to the Environment Agency) and obligations under the waste management licensing regime relinquished.

Waste Management Paper 26A describes in detail the procedures to be adopted to obtain a completion certificate; this procedure, however, is still in its infancy and very few landfill sites have progressed through to completion stage. The importance of keeping accurate records of site monitoring and the details of waste disposed of at a site are emphasised. It is important to liaise with the Environment Agency throughout the licensing and completion periods to make sure correct procedures are being adopted and current guidelines observed.

A primary requirement of the licensing regime is that a licence holder must be able to demonstrate that he/she is a 'fit-and-proper person'. This requires that the following three factors must be satisfied:

(a) that the licence holder (or other relevant person) has not been convicted of a relevant offence, **and**

(b) that the licensed activity is managed by a technically competent person (generally holding a relevant certificate of technical competence (COTC)) **and**

(c) that adequate financial provision has been made *'to discharge the obligations arising from the licence'*.

The preparation and submission of an application for a waste management licence is detailed in Waste Management Paper No 4 (WMP 4) [31]. A considerable amount of information is required and much of this is to be included within a Working Plan. This is prepared by the applicant, agreed with the regulator and details the infrastructures, waste management processes, pollution control measures and general matters of site management. It will also contain detailed design and operational statements explaining how the facility is to be developed. The applicant and the Environment Agency should usually begin discussions several months before the applicant submits this written application.

Licence applications are considered in a similar way to planning applications involving statutory consultations with various agencies and regulatory authorities, in relation to the proposed activities, location and time-scales, nature of wastes involved, etc.

The determination of waste management licence applications should, strictly speaking, be made within four months of the application date, as long as a relevant planning permission is already in place and all information is present and financial provisions have been thoroughly addressed. Again in common with planning applications, allowance is made in the relevant legislation [32] for an extension of this period, with the agreement of the Environment Agency and the Applicant.

In practice, applications for planning consents and waste management licences tend to be staggered, rather than concurrent, with applicants requiring the reassurance that a planning permission is likely to be forthcoming, before committing time and expenditure on a licensing application.

Once granted, waste management licences specify the activities which can be carried out and the land to which they relate. Conditions attached to the licence define, in detail, the way in which the activity shall be undertaken and will include *inter alia*, infrastructure, site preparation, waste reception, site operations, pollution control, site completion, monitoring and records.

A range of fees and charges are payable for:
- the initial licence application
- any modifications requested by the holder
- transfer to another holder
- annual 'subsistence' charges
- surrender.

The Environmental Protection Act 1990 revised the circumstances in which the holder of a waste management licence may surrender the licence. A licence cannot be surrendered unless the Agency is satisfied that the condition of the land is unlikely to cause pollution of the environment or harm to human health. An application for surrender would be made to the Agency and accompanied by a set of monitoring data and a completion report on the site, showing that the site meets with the completion conditions. If the Agency accepts the surrender a certificate of completion would be issued. These procedures are described in detail in Waste Management Paper No 26A *Landfill Completion*.

2.4.2 Special wastes

Certain waste materials are described as special wastes if they exhibit specified, hazardous properties. The Special Waste Regulations 1996 defines these properties and also provides a schedule of substances that are classified as special wastes. If a waste is recognised as a special waste, certain procedures for recording, handling and disposal, as described in the Special Waste Regulations, must be applied.

2.4.3 Exempt activities

The Waste Management Licensing Regulations 1994 describe, in Schedule 3, forty three activities which are exempt from waste management licensing. Activities are only exempt if they can be carried out in a manner which is consistent with the need to attain the 'relevant objectives' set out in Part 1 of Schedule 4 to the 1994 regulations. These include ensuring that waste is recovered or disposed of without:
- risk to water, air, soil, plants or animals
- causing nuisance through noise or odours
- adversely affecting the countryside or places of special interest.

In general the exemptions require that the waste is put to some (usually beneficial) use or are restricted to wastes or operations having little potential for environmental impact. These exempt activities span a wide variety of activities and a number may be particularly relevant to ground engineering projects. These are summarised as follows:

- Paragraph 7 – applies to application of waste, including soils, dredgings and certain other wastes, to agricultural land for its improvement

- Paragraph 9 – applies to spreading of wastes including soil, rock, ash and construction and demolition wastes in connection with land reclamation or improvements

- Paragraph 13 – the manufacture of soil materials from various construction, excavation and other waste materials

- Paragraph 15 – applies to the manufacture of aggregate/soil substitutes from wastes including construction and demolition wastes, tunnelling and excavation spoil, ash, slag, rock, etc.

- Paragraph 19 – applies to the storage and use of wastes, including construction and demolition wastes, tunnelling and excavation spoil, ash, slag, rock, etc., in works related to recreation and transport facilities

- Paragraph 24 – crushing, grinding or size reduction of bricks, tiles or concrete.

Sections 7 and 25 of the Schedule 3 provide exemptions for the disposal of dredgings for inland waterways. It should however be noted that a licence is required from MAFF for the disposal of dredgings at sea (see CIRIA Report 157, 1997) [33]

Most of the above contain restrictions as to where waste can be used or generated in order to stay within the exemption. They are all subject to restrictions and limitations which are detailed in Schedule 3. It is advisable to view the wording of these exemptions **strictly** and discuss intentions with the local Environment Agency staff well in advance of commencing any activity. Activities to which exemptions apply must be registered with the Agency, and will feature on a register of exempt activities. Certain activities may require registration with the District Council, for example concrete crushing, as an authorisation under Part 1 of the Environment Protection Act 1990 as a Part B process for local authority control. It is advisable to check with each authority where the proposed activity is to be conducted as it is understood that local authority attitudes vary.

2.4.4   Other activities

Section 16 of the Waste Management Licensing Regulations 1994 identifies various activities that are regulated by other legislation and therefore excluded from the waste management licensing regime. Apart from the discharge of liquid waste to sewers, which is regulated by the Water Resources Act 1991, none of the excluded activities would generally be applicable to ground engineering projects.

In order to comply with the Water Resources Act 1991 a construction project or associated landfill development may require discharge consent in addition to planning permission and a waste management licence. Under the Water Industry Act 1991 discharges to ground and surface watercourses are the responsibility of the Environment Agency while any disposal to sewers will require consent from the relevant sewerage authority.

2.5 WASTE MANAGEMENT LICENSING IN SCOTLAND

The waste management licensing regime in Scotland operates in a similar way to that operating in England and Wales. Specific differences from the regime operated in England and Wales include the following:

- The waste management licensing regime is enforced in Scotland by the Scottish Environment Protection Agency (SEPA)

- Formal waste management licensing is not required for activities carried out by waste disposal authorities (Islands or District Council), in which cases the activities are operated under a 'resolution' (an alternative less onerous option to a waste management licence: an agreed document specifying the activity method and issued by the relevant waste regulation authority).

- The deadline for the requirement for managers of waste management activities to hold a certificate of technical competence (COTC) has been extended in Scotland.

2.6 LANDFILL TAX

The landfill tax was introduced on 1 October 1996 and requires that all wastes (subject to certain exemptions), disposed of by way of landfill, are subject to the tax. The rate of tax upon its introduction was set by Customs and Excise as follows:

- £2 per tonne for 'inactive wastes', which are defined as including naturally occurring rocks and soils, ceramic or cemented materials and certain processed materials.

- £7 per tonne for other wastes.

Most excavated natural materials will be 'inactive wastes' for the purposes of the Landfill Tax, but occasions have arisen when naturally occurring materials have been classified as active or contaminated because of their chemical composition and would thus fall within the £7 per tonne category for 'other wastes'(see below); if there is any uncertainty regarding waste classification, guidance should be sought from the Environment Agency.

As contaminated material would be taxed at the higher rate, it is important to consider the tax implications of development in areas where contamination might be suspected. In this regard the contents of the Information Note 11/96 [34], provided by the HM Customs and Excise concerning contaminated land, should be noted. The scheduling of works could have tax implications if, for example, contaminated land clearance is not completed prior to site works. The Information Note in paragraph 1.4 provides guidance in this regard:

> *Expiry of exemption*
> *Where a reclamation is carried out to facilitate construction of a building or civil engineering work, the exemption will automatically expire, in respect of that part of the land which relates to the construction, when the construction, commences. For example, waste produced by excavating foundations will not qualify for the exemption. But waste produced during the clearing of pollutants from other parts of the same land will qualify providing the clearance is necessary to facilitate further development.*

The tax is levied on landfill operators at the point of disposal to landfill and is administered by HM Customs and Excise. However, these costs will ultimately be passed on to the relevant person responsible for the waste, e.g. client or contractor.

Exemption for certain specified types of waste have been permitted notably for contaminated land reclamation which, to qualify for the exemption, must meet the following conditions:

- the reclamation must be for one of the following reasons:
  - to reduce or remove pollutants so that the site can be developed, conserved, made into a public park or other amenity or used for agriculture or forestry; or
  - to reduce or remove the potential of pollutants to cause harm;
- where the activity giving rise to the pollution was carried out on land which is being reclaimed, the activity must have ceased [32].

Exemptions from landfill tax are also permitted for dredgings, and certain mining and quarrying wastes. HM Customs and Excise have recently issued A general guide to landfill tax 35 , which incorporates the eleven information notes and information Note 1/97 in relation to the reclamation of contaminated land 36. This note addresses some aspects of the uncertainty about the removal of contaminated material as part of construction on reclamation projects where 'spoil is removed in order to remove pollutants which would have to have been excavated in any case to level land or to dig foundations or service trenches. If we are (i.e. HM Customs and Excise) are satisfied that what is taking place is reclamation, then the waste arising from that work would all be exempt, even though it would have been removed in any case as part of the later construction.'

It would appear that the specified exemptions may not be permanent. For instance, the UK Government has recently promised to review the exemption for contaminated land within two years of introduction of the tax. [37].

2.7 DUTY OF CARE

All persons involved in waste management activities should be aware of their obligations as regards the duty of care for waste. Waste from *'works of construction or demolition'* are treated as industrial waste in the Environmental Protection Act 1990 and therefore subject to duty of care obligations [38]. The duty of care requires anyone who imports, produces, carries, keeps, treats or disposes of waste to ensure that the waste is managed in a correct manner.

The duty of care was introduced with the specific aim of reducing 'flytipping' (unauthorised disposals to land), by creating a system of responsibility for waste. Under the duty of care, waste producers must properly and securely store waste before ensuring that it is passed on to an authorised person, e.g. a registered waste carrier with the prescribed documentation (generally a controlled waste transfer note and waste description). Waste producers should satisfy themselves that the waste management facility, to which the waste is to be sent, is appropriately authorised to take the waste and is dealing with it lawfully.

2.8 FURTHER LEGISLATIVE CONTROLS ON WASTE REGULATION

The current waste management planning and licensing regime is a relatively new one. Alongside this regime, a series of legislative controls have been established which, while not specifically aiming to control the impact of waste management practices, nevertheless are applicable in certain circumstances. The Environment Agency or local planning authority will be able to advise in specific cases. These additional controls are briefly discussed below.

2.8.1   Statutory nuisance

Statutory nuisance provisions 39 require the control of any smoke, fumes, gases, dust, smell, steam noise or other effluvia, etc. or accumulation which is 'prejudicial to health or a nuisance'. The meaning of the term statutory nuisance is not explicitly defined in the legislation and as such its applicability is heavily dependent on case law. However action under breaches of statutory nuisance controls have been successfully won against a variety of waste management activities, e.g. dust blown from stockpiles, or excessive noise.

2.8.2   Common law

Waste management activities are indirectly covered by common law (civil offences as opposed to criminal offences). Common law allows action to be taken by individuals for pollution caused by activities giving rise in particular to trespass, nuisance or negligence. Two specific cases provide the corner-stone for common law; Rylands v Fletcher 1868 and Cambridge Water Company v Eastern Counties Leather 1993. In general, the level of proof required to be presented for common law cases is lower than would be required under criminal law and, as such, can provide a relatively effective system for individuals.

2.8.3   Water control legislation

The Water Resources Act 1991 is the principal statutory control for the protection of water. This act states that it is an offence to permit the entry of any poisonous, noxious or polluting matter (including solid waste) into controlled waters. Controlled waters [40], as defined in the Act, include all groundwater and inland waters and estuaries.

2.9   GUIDANCE ON TECHNICAL ASPECTS OF WASTE MANAGEMENT

The prime source of guidance on **technical** aspects of waste management is the Environment Agency, and comes in the form of Waste Management Papers (WMPs). The WMP series comprises guidance on specific aspects of waste management (e.g. landfill engineering) or on specific types of waste. Some of the WMPs are statutory guidance, and as such must be followed by the relevant regulator(s). The WMP series also provides a valuable source of information for other parties involved in waste management activities. The most important WMPs in relation to the management of ground engineering waste are as follows:

- WMP4 *The Licensing of Waste Facilities* (1994) [31]
- WMP23 *Special Wastes* (in preparation 1996) [41]
- WMP26 Series (A-E) (1993, etc.), particularly WMP26B *Landfill design, construction and operational practice* [42]
- WMP27 *Landfill Gas* [43].

2.10   WASTE MANAGEMENT IN GROUND ENGINEERING

Waste management can have an impact on both the technical and the economic feasibility of a project. This is particularly the case in ground engineering projects where arisings can be substantial and disposal costs can be a significant proportion of contract costs. Furthermore there is now a substantial body of legislation which introduces a series of technical and economic hurdles that need to be overcome before the necessary authorisations are obtained to allow waste disposal to proceed. The publication of the UK Government's Waste Strategy, and more particularly the cost penalties arising from the implementation of the landfill tax, has further focused attention on waste minimisation.

It is therefore essential that waste management is given an appropriate profile at all stages of a project from its formulation and outline design, through the tendering process and to project implementation. The various matters that may be considered to improve the management of spoil throughout the life of a project are outlined in Section 6.1 and in Figures 6.1 to 6.4 inclusive.

3 Spoil management practice

At present, construction and demolition account for the second largest component volume of controlled wastes in the UK [3]. (The largest source is industrial). Surplus spoil material from a construction project can form the main constituent of the waste stream.

The disposal of excavation material is being given higher priority as landfill capacity becomes more scarce and more costly. Spoil minimisation, reuse and recycling are therefore beneficial concepts in both economic and environmental terms. As such, there is increasing pressure to identify alternative uses or routes for the disposal of spoil. It is critical, however, that such uses and disposal routes are sound in engineering, planning and environmental terms and do not compromise waste management regulations.

This section addresses current and emerging practices in the management of ground engineering spoil. Examples of site practice are included, where the volume of spoil generated is minimised, while maximising the volume of spoil that is reused or recycled on and off site for ancillary purposes. The spoil considered is that generated from three types of engineering works: general construction spoil, dredged material and tunnelling spoil. Within each of these engineering operations, the incorporation of spoil into the works or its disposal off site is examined.

Emphasis is placed upon:

- consideration of spoil during the design and construction stages of the ground engineering operation
- financial restraints and legal/planning requirements
- methods for reducing, reusing and recycling of spoil.

For the uses and disposal routes identified, the associated advantages and constraints are discussed in terms of engineering applicability, e.g. whether the option is only suitable for particular materials, the economics of adopting the method, the environmental impacts, relevant legislation or the timing of the project.

An environmental impact is the change in an environmental parameter resulting from a particular activity when compared with the situation which would have occurred had the activity not been initiated. Some environmental impacts resulting from the disposal of ground engineering spoil can be quantified, e.g. the increase in noise or air pollution attributed to the related vehicle and haulage movements; others are not quantifiable, e.g. the provision of visual screening resulting from the disposal of spoil.

3.1 THE ROLES OF CLIENT, DESIGNER AND CONTRACTOR

By writing it into the brief, the client can stipulate from the outset of the project that the designer give careful consideration to spoil creation and its after-use. The brief may also identify possible reuse or disposal measures. For example, it could identify adjacent land which would benefit from being landscaped using surplus spoil or land on which materials may be stored for reuse on or off the site. These measures can reduce the cost of the project.

Design, although only one of the factors influencing the volume of construction waste produced, can influence the disposal method used (either on or off site). If consideration is given to spoil reduction at the concept stage and integrated as an essential part of a design, the amount of spoil sent to landfill can be reduced. A key area of influence for designers in terms of spoil creation, therefore, is to design and specify schemes such that there is minimisation of the amount of surplus spoil produced or the adoption of alternative construction methods. At this early stage, designers should also consider how the spoil material can be reused and recycled effectively, both on and off site.

The role that both main and sub-contractors play in minimising the volume of excavated spoil in the traditional construction-only contract is, to a certain extent, limited by their late entry into projects. However, on most construction projects, the contractor chooses the construction techniques and practices. These choices can strongly influence the amount of material that is suitable for reuse.

Contracts are increasingly being carried out on a design/build/finance/operate (DBFO) basis. In that both the design and the construction works are under a single control, there is more opportunity to co-ordinate spoil reduction measures. Although there is more scope within the DBFO contract than with standard contracts to reduce the quantity of surplus spoil, practitioners are of the view that the opportunity for the designer/contractor to make major changes to the earthworks in a DBFO contract is sometimes limited. This is because of constraints on changing spoil volumes, e.g. the design, once approved, has fixed the vertical/horizontal alignments. If a decision is taken by the designer/contractor to vary the outline design, standards may be infringed and additional land may be required. These difficulties could be overcome if the client was able to give the designer and the DBFO contractor greater flexibility to consider spoil reduction, e.g. the provision of a flexible outline design giving greater scope to achieve a balance between cut and fill.

The following section highlights current on-site practices which aim to minimise the volume of spoil created and identifies various approaches for reusing or recycling spoil. Reference should also be made to the series of CIRIA Reports on waste minisation and recycling in construction [44-47].

3.2 MINIMISING VOLUMES OF SPOIL GENERATED

3.2.1 Balancing cut with fill

Cut and fill is the method by which the ground is lowered or raised in order to create a more level platform, most typically in roadworks. The priority therefore is to define the alignment, location, levels and gradients which will most nearly balance the volumes of re-usable cut-and-fill materials. Adjustments to the vertical alignment should apply to cross-sections as well as longitudinally. A balance in the volumes of cut and fill is desirable both in economic terms and as a means of limiting interference with the surrounding area. Inevitably there will be occasions where this cannot be achieved and quantities of suitable material may have to be imported to, or exported from, the site in addition to disposing of unsuitable soils. The transport of large volumes of material to and from the site has clear environmental impacts from increased air and noise pollution and disturbance to local residents.

The current trend is to lower the road and rail alignments in order to reduce visual and noise impacts. This makes it more difficult to balance cut-and-fill volumes. Increasing the use of landscaping embankments can redress the balance. Therefore when designing a transport corridor consideration could be given to a lateral balance of cut and fill in addition to the traditional long-section balance (see Section 3.3). The balancing of cut and fill is not only a significant aspect of road and rail design but is applicable to all construction. It is particularly relevant to developments that are sited on hillsides or sloping ground.

Reduction of the steepness of cutting and embankment slopes can improve the visual impact. A further advantage of this can be the return of land to agriculture, thus minimising permanent land-take; slopes of 1(V): 5(H) or gentler can be used in this way. The use of a less steep slope produces more spoil from cuttings and uses more spoil in embankments. In some circumstances the use of a less steep slope will aid the fill balance, in others it will make it worse.

The splitting of carriageways on dual carriageway road schemes in hilly terrain can make substantial savings in spoil generation, improving the stability of sidelong ground and the visual appearance of the scheme. Examples of this are the M6 in Cumbria, (see Figure 3.1) the M2 in Kent, and the A74/M74 in Glasgow.

The same type of solution can also be applied to building developments on sloping sites.

Figure 3.1 Grade separation on the M6 motorway

3.2.2 Ground treatment

The *in-situ* treatment of weak soils and fills can improve their strength and compressibility characteristics. This can avoid excavation of the poor ground or the need to remove it from site or it allows for the use of an alternative design method.

Ground treatment is a wide subject and detailed descriptions of the methods available would not be appropriate for this report. Methods which should be considered include:

- dynamic compaction
- vibro-compaction
- vibro-replacement
- preloading and surcharging
- wick drains
- soil nailing
- lime and lime-cement columns
- deep *in-situ* mixing.

3.2.3 Stabilisation

The stabilisation of soils involves the application of an additive to improve materials which would otherwise not be acceptable for use on site (Figure 3.2). It can therefore reduce both the need to remove large volumes of unsuitable material from site and the need for imported fill.

Figure 3.2 Lime stabilisation

Methods of soil stabilisation include, but are not limited to, the following operations:

- incorporating lime into the soil
- mixing cement with the soil

Even adding relatively small dosages of quicklime to fill materials too wet otherwise to be used can render them suitable. Clayey subgrades can be improved, thereby avoiding or reducing the import of granular materials for use as capping.

Suitable soil types for lime stabilisation. The primary use of lime [48] is in the treatment of clayey soils, although a wide range of soils from clayey gravels through to clays may benefit from its application. For full stabilisation, soils need a reactive clay content of over 10%. Where silt predominates, moisture susceptibility can be reduced, although little pozzolanic strengthening will develop. The effectiveness is therefore dependent on the nature of the soils and where soils react well, small and economic use of lime can be made.

The proportion of lime required in any particular application can be determined [49] through laboratory testing in accordance with BS1924.

Typically after treatment there is:

- an increase in strength and bearing capacity
- a reduction of the soil's susceptibility to swell and shrink
- a reduction in the water content of the soil as the lime hydrates, which leads to improved strength, workability and compaction characteristics.

In a recent road contract, up to 100 000 m^3 of soft silt, classified as being unsuitable, was modified on-site by mixing with lime and was then incorporated into the permanent works [47].

Note that soils with high sulphate contents and substantial reactive clay content are not suitable for lime stabilisation.

Cement stabilisation. Cement stabilisation of road subgrade soils is generally used where the soil is fine grained but mainly granular and where locally occurring deposits of gravel or rock for use as capping or sub-base are scarce.

3.2.4   Construction methods

Construction methods employed in earthworks operations can have a significant effect upon the suitability of excavated (cut) materials for reuse on the site as fill, notably in embankments. Examples of relevant excavation and deposition effects are:

- earthworks timing, e.g. to avoid wet weather and work in earthworks 'seasons'
- choice of excavation equipment and transportation methods, e.g. using a face shovel to excavate chalk
- drainage of cut areas, avoidance of ponding and soil softening
- fill compaction with minimal delay especially in wet weather conditions
- fill profiling, efficient drainage during and after filling.

If, despite the above measures, the material is or becomes unsuitable for earthworks, having too high a moisture content, it is sometimes possible to allow the material to dry to the extent that it can be used. Drying can be achieved (depending on the nature of the materials) by either stockpiling or, in dry weather conditions, spreading the material in the fill area as loose layers or in windrows and allowing it to dry before compaction. Stockpiling necessitates double handling and is only effective if the material is sufficiently free draining.

Construction methods, such as the use of piling, vibro-concrete columns, staged construction and lightweight fill in embankments can result in the leaving in place of soils which might otherwise have to be removed as spoil. The installation method of piling will affect the amount of spoil generated. Bored piling involves the need to dispose of generated spoil, but if driven piles are used the soil is displaced thereby eliminating the creation of spoil. In some circumstances it is convenient to use displacement bored piles. These form the pile bore by augering temporary pile casing into the ground and laterally compacting the soil rather than bringing spoil to the surface.

3.2.5 Specifications for earthworks

On occasion, potential waste materials are only marginally unsuitable for use in earthworks. In such situations a minor relaxation or modification to the standard earthworks specifications would avoid the creation of waste materials. Any such changes would require the agreement of the client and may involve the adoption of conservative design methods. If a material is not acceptable for highway embankment fill (for example under the DoT Specification for Highway Works), the designer could set appropriate limits for the material to be acceptable as landscape fill.

3.2.6 No-dig technology

The traditional approach to pipe-laying has been to excavate and backfill trenches. Various alternatives are now available, including the use of micro-tunnelling techniques. An advantage over conventional trenching methods is that they reduce the excavation of surfaced areas which would subsequently need disposal and replacement. Economic considerations determine when the no-dig method is adopted and at present only 2% of installations in the UK have been carried out using this method. Some utility companies are now stipulating that, where possible, all installations are carried out by this method [50].

3.2.7 Containment of contaminated land to avoid removal

In many projects there is the requirement for the removal of large volumes of contaminated or unsuitable material followed by the importation of replacement material. However, it is sometimes possible to avoid its removal by containing the contaminated material *in situ*. A number of factors, which include cost and methods of capping and containment, will determine whether this option is a viable alternative to disposal off-site. The geology of the site and the proposed after-use will also determine which type of containment cell, if any, is appropriate. Although there is no requirement for a licence if the contaminated material remains on site, the Environment Agency strongly recommends that they are contacted during the initial stages of the project so that they may advise on barrier type. Table 3.1 lists types of in-ground barrier and their potential advantages as disadvantages.

The Environment Agency advises that when selling the land on the seller should disclose all details regarding the history of the site prior to the sale such as the extent of contamination, the type of contamination, details of containment, ground investigation and testing results and the outcome of any other investigations undertaken. If all details are disclosed prior to sale, the liability is passed onto the buyer. To strengthen this position further, the Environment Agency recommend that a contract be drawn up between the parties to this effect. If the land is not sold on, and a problem occurs at a later date, all the parties involved are liable. Hence all parties should make themselves aware of their long-term liabilities concerning contaminated land.

3.2.8 Treatment of contaminated land to avoid removal

The technology associated with the *in-situ* treatment of contaminated soils is developing rapidly. *In-situ* treatment is not at present employed on a widespread basis; the increased adoption of such methods will depend upon their costs and environmental benefits compared with the costs and viability of removal or containment, the two methods most used. However, it is very likely that environmental pressures and the increased costs of removal will cause *in-situ* treatment, both small scale and large scale, to be used more often. Another type of treatment involves removal, although not necessarily from the site.

For example, a system of soil washing is currently in use in Germany and the USA. The process involves sieving, sorting, crushing and washing the soil before passing it into bioreactor vessels as slurry. The clean soil slurry is dewatered and the water recycled into the process [51]. This is an *ex-situ* method. CIRIA Special Publication 107, *Remedial treatment for contaminated land* also contain information about soil washing. [57]

Table 3.1 Potential advantages and disadvantages of in-ground barrier types (from K. Privett *et al.*, [52]).

Barrier type	Potential advantages	Potential disadvantages
Cut-and-fill barrier	can be constructed in most types of ground including rock	may involve excavation of potentially contaminated soil
Displacement barrier	does not involve excavation of potentially contaminated soil	the presence of boulders, rocks or bulky waste may impede installation depth of penetration
		very dependent on soil type incapable of forming a deep key into rock
Mix-in-place barrier	does not involve excavation of potentially contaminated soil	performance depends on soil type
	can be constructed in most types of ground including rock	
Injected barrier	does not involve excavation of potentially contaminated soil	very dependent on soil type

3.3 THE USE OF SPOIL ON SITE THROUGH LAND REPROFILING AND RAISING

The definition of land reprofiling and land raising is the controlled deposit of spoil on land to produce a new landform. This option is therefore applicable to both on-site and off-site disposal. Low-lying areas on the site could be raised with a view to developing them in the future. If adjacent land is held this should be identified in the brief, as it could be landscaped using excavated spoil or used for storing spoil for reuse on or off site. However, as with all earthworks projects, careful planning is needed (and necessary planning permissions and waste management licences sought, see Section 2) in order to avoid as far as possible the necessity for temporary spoil-heaps and the consequent double handling.

Through the adoption of a flexible earthworks/landscape design it is possible significantly to reduce costs at the construction phase. For example, a flexible landscape design can react to changes in spoil volumes created by the actual site conditions differing from those assumed during design. Planning permission is a necessary part of this so that variable heights of mounding may be incorporated on site if more material becomes available.

Noise bunds, visual barriers and features such as roundabouts often use excavated spoil from the site. Consideration should be given to the use of spoil in this manner and whether, given land restrictions, the side slopes of embankments may be reduced in order to incorporate more spoil. If the slope of the embankment is slackened to 1(V) in 5(H) or less, it can be returned to agricultural use and enables the bunds to blend into the countryside. This also reduces the permanent land-take.

3.4   METHODS OF IMPROVING SPOIL

Spoil unsuitable in its state as excavated material, if appropriately treated, will become amenable to beneficial use on site. The spoil, when treated, must satisfy the specified material standard for the proposed use.

3.4.1   Spoil handling

The potential for improving spoil is enhanced if different types of spoil, as far as possible, are kept separate in the spoil handling and storage operations. In addition spoil sometimes can be improved by screening to provide materials of suitable grading.

3.4.2   Soil reinforcement

A wide range of civil engineering structures use reinforced soil; examples include vertical reinforced soil walls and abutments, steep-sided embankments and cuttings, slope stabilisation and basal reinforcement of foundations for structures constructed on soft ground. Other applications where reinforced soil has been used include landscape features, flood embankment structures, dock walls, landfill cells to maximise void space, temporary works and foundations for earthworks. The main benefit of using reinforced earth techniques is the reduction in the volumes of fill required for embankments.

To give one example, a contractor achieved major cost savings through the use of reinforced soil in cuttings during works on the M25 widening in Surrey, as they were able to reuse the as-dug materials in providing steepened slopes. With the construction and disposal methods originally proposed, as least 50 000 m^3 of spoil would have had to be removed to a landfill site [53].

3.4.3   Soil layering

Soil layering is a technique employed where the susceptibility of excavated material to moisture change may prevent it being used as fill. It involves the use of wet, but otherwise suitable, material in embankments, placing it between drainage layers with a layer of dry material laid and compacted on top in the normal manner. The adoption of this technique during the construction of road embankments for part of the M6 was especially important because it was necessary to reuse excavated material, since there were few local sources of suitable imported fill and the creation of borrow pits was not permitted.

3.4.4 Soil additives

As well as the in-situ stabilisation of subgrades by lime and cement which avoids the generation of spoil, otherwise unsuitable materials can be improved by mixing with these additives. Thus the drying properties of lime assist the dewatering of slurries, making them easier to transport and their disposal often cheaper. Similarly lime can be mixed into softened clays fills.

3.5 OFF-SITE OPTIONS

The use of spoil off site has implications in terms of transportation costs and environmental impacts. These would have to be assessed as part of the submission of the planning application for the works. When considering how spoil may be put to a beneficial use off site it is important to consider the environmental impact of the transportation of that spoil. For example, if a landfill is located near the site and a potential use is further afield, which is the better option in terms of environmental impact and financial cost?

3.5.1 Reclamation of quarries and borrow pits

The disposal of ground engineering spoil is sometimes possible in excavations left by the extraction of minerals such as sand and gravel. This an attractive solution wherever it is feasible, but unfortunately it is rarely a viable option. Apart from the possibility that placing spoil in this manner may cause pollution of underground water supplies, ground engineering works are rarely sufficiently close to suitable excavations for this form of disposal to be an economic proposition. Transport of materials is the most inhibiting factor. Haulage costs are a function of the quantity of material and the haulage distance: they bear no relation to the value of the material that is being carried.

The backfilling of surplus materials to disused quarry sites will require planning consent and a waste management licence, and an environmental impact assessment would have to be submitted with the planning application. In addition to the cost implications, advanced timing is also necessary as it may be a matter of months (or even years, if it is a particularly contentious site) before planning permission is granted.

In 1986 the Engineer for the Warminster Bypass, approached local planning authority officials to discuss the disposal of spoil from the project. Adjacent to the route, three chalk borrow pits were located; the chalk extracted was used in the construction of the road capping layer. Permission was sought from the local planning authority to dispose of the unsuitable spoil generated on the road construction site in the borrow pits. An agreement was reached whereby the borrow pits were reinstated to the former level of the land: permission was granted by the local planning authority as it was deemed that no material change of land use had occurred. As outlined in Section 2, waste regulations have altered since 1986, and planning regulations have been tightened. Therefore, it is likely that such a project taking place today would have to register an exemption from waste management licensing and obtain formal planning permission in order to dispose of the surplus excavation spoil in this way.

3.5.2 Spoil exchange

There is substantial scope for materials exchanges within the construction industry; the advantages of using excess spoil from one construction site at another are:

• avoidance of primary material usage

- reduced need for borrow pits

- avoidance of disposal of excess spoil to landfill and therefore less take-up of landfill space

- net cost savings to each site.

Removal of spoil from one site to another must conform with current legislation, as identified in Section 2.

In exchanging surplus materials, it is important that all parties involved, from the client to the designer to the contractor, take into account the benefits of exchanging spoil when making decisions about a project. Although a direct comparison between environmental effects and actual costs is not easy and each project is unique, there are significant benefits from exchanging spoil. Such benefits include savings with regard to landfill tax and landfill space, borrow is minimised, and what was once considered waste at one site is a valuable resource at another.

Possible disadvantages and problems associated with spoil exchange include:

- haulage costs increasing

- project timings not coinciding

- double handling of spoil.

Spoil exchange is frequently severely limited by the non-availability of suitable materials within an economic haulage distance. Combined with this is the fact that fill is often composed of relatively low-grade material which means that transport costs are the predominant factor in the economics of imported fill. For this reason the haulage distances of fill materials have to be short. The timing of the projects also is critical, with surplus spoil being available at one site when bulk fill is required at another. Delay in the delivery of material can incur increased project costs and would not be acceptable in view of the limited periods in which earthworks can be carried out. The timing of the delivery of exchange spoil may mean that it will have to be temporarily stockpiled. This would cause difficulty if land is restricted and works are being conducted in a confined space. It also incurs double handling and will, if use is being made of an intermediate site, require an additional planning application, and perhaps additional handling, and the risk of the material degrading.

However, despite these difficulties, it is likely that the exchanging of spoil will increase as landfilling costs rise and environmental factors receive more attention. It should be feasible for landfill sites to be used as waste exchange sites where surplus spoil could be stockpiled and sold on when required. This could solve the timing problem referred to above. The co-ordination of spoil exchange could be managed by a governmental or non-governmental database and the availability and requirements of spoil for exchange could be advertised in the trade press and on the Internet.

The Civil Engineering Department of the Hong Kong Government maintains a database primarily containing details of public sector construction projects although it also includes the larger private sector schemes. The database contains details of the construction programme and requirements for fill and spoil expectations including spoil type. The objective of the database is to indicate projects with surplus spoil and those that require additional bulk fill thereby facilitating the exchange of spoil.

Informal spoil exchanges, similar to the Hong Kong example, have been established in the UK. In Warrington New Town a spoil exchange system was operated during its earlier development.

The questionnaires returned for this study identified four sites that had exchanged spoil, see Section 4.6. None of these projects had considered spoil exchange at the planning stage.

3.5.3 Land improvement

Spoil surplus to the requirements of a project can be used to improve the surrounding land by in-filling and levelling hollows. If possible, the ground contours should be planned so that agricultural development can continue on completion of the filling. Such an approach requires advanced discussions with occupiers of surrounding land and requires planning permission.

Good quality, uncontaminated soils are often in high demand in urban areas and achieve good prices, therefore justifying longer haulage distances. Materials like top soil are valuable, but supply and demand are out of balance. The inevitable mismatch between the timing and supply and demand of soil, could be overcome if storage facilities were available. Normally such facilities do not exist and therefore financial incentives govern to a large extent whether the price at the point of sale justifies the transport cost.

3.5.4 Landfill engineering

Landfill operators may welcome spoil for their 'landfill engineering', i.e. for bunds and daily cover layers. Thus the spoil from a construction project may be economically attractive to a landfill operator looking for sources of materials.

3.6 DREDGED MATERIALS

Attitudes towards dredged material are changing; there is a tendency to see it more as a resource than a waste. The possible beneficial use of dredgings depends on a number of factors which include: the physical nature of the dredged material, its contaminant status, the volume to be dredged, the geographical location, and the type of dredging equipment used. CIRIA Report 157 [33] provides guidance on the disposal of dredgings to land.

Dredged materials are most commonly employed for reclamation and land-raising works, often involving large volumes of material; they normally require the use of ground improvement techniques or the adoption of piled foundations to enable subsequent construction works to take place.

There are many possible uses for sands and gravels, but finding beneficial uses for dredged silts, which form the majority of maintenance dredging in the UK, is much more difficult.

Surplus uncontaminated dredgings for marine projects may be disposed at sea provided a MAFF licence can be obtained. Otherwise surplus dredged material is taken to landfill.

Where dredgings are too contaminated to be disposed, the coarse fraction, if separated (using a hydrocyclone separator), may be cleaned to a standard whereby it can be used. Currently however, the majority of contaminated dredged material is sent to landfill.

The contractor working on the A13 dual carriageway in Essex identified a method whereby silt which was originally designated as being an unsuitable material and destined to be taken off site was kept on site and used as embankment fill. The silt, excavated from the existing lagoons through which the route of the new road runs, was mixed with lime and PFA before being incorporated into embankment structures. A volume of 230 000 m^3 of modified material was eventually used in the embankments out of a total of 1.6 million m^3.

3.7 SPOIL FROM TUNNELLING

Excavation of tunnels takes place in various types of ground, ranging from made ground, sand, gravel, clay and shale, through to hard rocks. Contractors therefore use the excavated spoil for a variety of purposes. In addition, the type of excavation method employed and engineering equipment used to extract the spoil will also influence the after-use of the material. For example, in some instances the material extracted will be dry and in others a liquid slurry will be produced.

Excavated rock from other tunnelling projects have been used for purposes such as coastal protection works and occasionally for use as aggregates.

During tunnelling on the UK side for the Channel Tunnel, the 14 000 tonnes per day of excavated chalk marl were transformed into 40 hectares of wildlife and amenity land located at the foot of Shakespeare Cliff (Figure 3.3). The size of this project and its potentially astronomical waste disposal costs, provided the primary impetus for this parkland development.

Liquid spoils or slurries incur higher costs as they are more difficult to transport and can only be disposed to landfills that accept liquid waste. This was a problem faced by contractors on the Jubilee Line Extension project. Here liquid spoil was acceptable in that it was easy convey to it from the tunnel, but solid spoil was preferred for disposal as being easier to transport and dispose of more cost-effectively. Slurry can be de-watered by allowing it to settle in lagoons (if the site area is large enough for lagoons). In some instances, after settling in lagoons has taken place, the waste material has then been used for landscaping purposes. If there is no space for lagoons, partial dewatering can be achieved using hydrocyclones. Alternatively, the slurry may be stabilised by use of additives, refer to Section 3.2.3

3.8 ROLES IN SPOIL REDUCTION

Reduction in the volume of spoil which is disposed to landfill is the responsibility of clients, designers and contractors. Professionals from each of these groups are involved at different stages of the project programme; each has a role in reducing the amount of spoil disposed to landfill.

At the initial stage, the client exerts considerable control. This influence on the project stems from including spoil reduction and disposal measures in the design brief. Later these should become specified in the tender documents. The designer, by determining the project design, and by giving careful consideration to the reuse and recycling of spoil, has an important input. The contractor has less scope to influence the amount of spoil generated. However, the contractor, by adopting techniques which involve reusing or recycling spoil has a significant part to play in reducing the volume of spoil sent to landfill.

Figure 3.3 Reclamation with Channel Tunnel spoil, Shakespeare Cliff, Dover

4   The questionnaire survey

4.1   AIM OF THE SURVEY

The questionnaire survey was intended to provide a broad view of UK practice in the reuse, recycling and disposal of excavated and surplus ground materials generated from civil engineering operations. The relatively small number and diversity of the projects surveyed meant that it was not appropriate to attempt to derive statistical relations from the results.

The survey targeted civil engineering projects that generated different types, forms and quantities of spoil. The three main parties involved in each project i.e. the client, engineer and the contractor, were approached in the summer of 1996, and asked to reply to the questionnaire within one month. In practice replies came back over several months, up to the beginning of 1997.

The questionnaires used in this survey were designed to examine the influence of the nature, forms and quantity of spoil on the chosen disposal, reuse and recycling options. As client, engineer and contractor differ in their roles and levels of involvement in a project, separate questionnaires were prepared. Each of these had its own emphasis.

- The client's questionnaire – overall planning of the project

- The engineer's questionnaire – planning and execution of the ground engineering operations

- The contractor's questionnaire – execution of disposal, reuse and recycling of spoil

4.2   TYPE OF CONSTRUCTION PROJECT SURVEY

Respondents to the questionnaire provided information on 32 sites (representing 80% of the forty targeted projects). These comprised eight different types of civil engineering projects, i.e. roads, reclamation/remediation, landfill construction, commercial development, wastewater and water treatment works, tunnels, and a power station construction. Appendix 1, Tables A1.1 and A1.2, present summary information about the projects in terms of type of construction project, total cost, their scope, ground conditions, ground engineering operations, spoil generation, reuse and disposal, etc.

4.3   RESPONSE AND LEVEL OF RETURNS

Three questionnaires were sent to each of the forty projects identified, i.e. to the Client, the Engineer and the Contractor of each. Overall, there were 64 returns, a response rate of 53%, being 16 from the clients (40%), and 25 from engineers (62%) and 23 from contractors (57%).

4.4   RESULTS RELATING TO TYPE OF PROJECT AND TYPES OF SPOIL

4.4.1   Types and scale of ground engineering operations

In the 32 projects for which there were returned questionnaires, there were 28 different types of ground engineering operation, ranging from topsoil stripping to jet grouting. These are presented in Table A1.2 in Appendix 1. The most frequent was open (i.e. unsupported) excavation, i.e. the general excavation to remove ground or to reduce the ground level. Even in these relatively few projects, it was apparent that the nature of the project determines the type of ground engineering operations used. For example cut-and-fill earthworks and trench excavation, as would be expected, are the most common ground engineering operations in road works.

The ground engineering operations in the 25 projects for which costs were given had total costs of between £0.25M and £7M, but mainly from £1M to £2M. These made up only a small proportion of total project cost, i.e. from 1 to 10% (Table A1.2 in Appendix 1).

Typically for these projects the ground engineering operations were over an initial 1 to 3 months, although a few took place over more than two years.

4.4.2   Types and volumes of spoil

The volume of spoil generated from the projects ranged from as little as 1400 to 3000 000 m^3. Some two-thirds, however, were less than 300 000 m^3 (Figure 4.1). As might be expected, six of the eight largest were on roadworks projects.

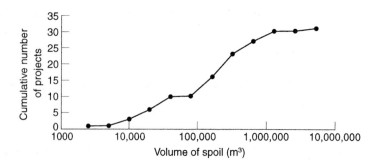

Figure 4.1 Distribution of volumes of spoil on the projects

The geological characteristics of the sites are typical of the range of drift and solid geologies found from Sussex in the south to the Lancashire coast and Newcastle-upon-Tyne in the north. There are summaries of the geology of the sites in Table A1.1 of Appendix 1. Hence the excavated materials include:

- various types of made ground, including municipal solid waste
- surficial deposits, such as alluvial clays, glacial tills, terrace gravels, head, etc.
- overconsolidated clays, e.g. London, Oxford and Lias Clays
- weak and weathered rocks, e.g. chalk, mudstones, shales
- hard rocks, e.g. siltstones, sandstones.

While specific equipment is used to excavate the ground in particular operations (e.g. the auger rig for large-diameter bored piling), there was widespread use of backacters for all types of general excavation, i.e. whether for trenching, cut-and-fill operations, etc., coupled with use of lorries and dump trucks to transport the spoil. Scrapers are little used now in UK for muck-shifting because articulated dump trunks and backacters are more flexible.

The questionnaire asked respondents to classify the spoil by one of three descriptions, i.e.

- D (meaning in a dry form): large blocks, mixed-size lumps, powdery, or otherwise in a dry form, e.g. boulders, rubble

- W (meaning in a wet form): mixture of lumps and mud, slurry

- M: (meaning in a mixed form) mixed materials, e.g. ground spoil mixed with bentonite slurry, lime, PFA, etc.

There were roughly equal numbers of the separately identified spoil materials classed as either D or W (40% of each) with some 20% of class M. In volume terms, however, the proportions were: D 69%; W 24%; and M 7%. The mixed materials tended to be associated with the specialist geotechnical works, e.g. diaphragm walling.

Although there was a substantial proportion of what was classed as W (i.e. wet) spoil, much of that was free draining sand and gravel. Other than the site remediation projects, which essentially are about treatment of the excavated material, only four other projects treated surplus spoil in some way prior either to reuse or disposal, i.e.

- the removal of timber and other debris from made ground

- drying of soft clay spoil and stockpiling sand for it to drain prior to their reuse

- drying of spoil from an earth pressure balance tunnelling machine advancing through mixed faces of glacial sands and boulder clays prior to reuse elsewhere

- addition of lime to canal dredgings prior to their transport to a disposal site.

The cost of these treatments of spoil – while small when compared to the total project cost – can be quite a substantial proportion of the ground engineering cost.

4.5   RESULTS RELATING TO DISPOSAL ROUTE AND DESTINATION

About one fifth of the projects reused all of their spoil. Thus, there was surplus spoil available on about 80% of the sites, and 25% of these disposed all spoil to landfill.

Some of the survey results show how the volume of surplus spoil sent to landfill can depend on the nature of the project. For example, the two commercial developments sent all of their spoil to landfill off site. Projects such as these would have little or no stockpile space available on site nor reuse opportunities in the project for the spoil. As well as the quantities being relatively small (and this is also a reason why landfill disposal is the default option), the spoil is likely to be a mixture of surface soils, e.g. made ground, and probably unsuitable for use by others. Road schemes (except perhaps urban roads almost wholly in cut), wastewater treatment plants, pipelines, quarry/landfill and other site remediation projects, however, are likely to have greater space for spoil storage and for on-site reuse, e.g. as noise barriers and landscaping embankments. Thus these types of projects may have less need to dispose surplus spoil to landfill – but, if they do , the quantities are likely to be much greater than those of building developments.

The landfills used for disposal off site were commercially operated. Three of the projects, including two reclamation projects, constructed their own on-site disposal cells.

4.6 RESULTS RELATING TO REUSE

While 21 of the 32 projects of this survey reused some of their surplus spoil on site (Table 4.1), 12 also found off-site uses for their surplus. Four projects reported that they had participated in spoil exchange schemes (Table 4.2).

Table 4.1 Reuse of surplus spoil

Project types	Number of projects and type of reuse			
	On-site		Off-site	
Roads	7	Embankment Landscape	5	Not known
Site remediations	6	Fill Slope reprofiling Backfill Landscaping	3	Capping for other landfill
Power station	1	Backfill	0	-
Commercial development	0	-	0	-
Wastewater/ water treatment plants	3	Backfill Landscaping	1	Landscaping for other projects
Quarry and landfill construction	2	Clay lining for cell	2	Landscaping
Tunnel	0	-	1	Landscaping
Dredging	1	Landscaping	0	-
Pipeline	1	Backfill for easement	0	-
Total	21	-	12	-

Table 4.2 Participation in a spoil exchange scheme (both transfer and receipt)

Projects	Replies as to whether the project has participated in a spoil exchange scheme		
	Yes	No	NA
Road	1	6	2
Site remediation project	3	6	1
Power station	0	1	0
Commercial development	0	0	2
Wastewater and water treatment plant	0	3	0
Quarry and landfill construction	0	2	0
Tunnel	0	1	0
Dredging	0	1	0
Pipeline	0	0	1
Total	4	20	6

NA: No answer given

The most common reuse options were landscaping and amenity or mitigation embankments on site (Table 4.1). These provide flexibility for the contractor's programme, relatively low handling and transport costs, and do not incur staff costs in finding and following up possible off-site markets.

4.7   RESULTS RELATING TO COSTS

The costs of dealing with surplus spoil tend, on most construction projects, to be a relatively small proportion of the total project cost, i.e. from less than 1 to about 5% of the total. (Table 4.3 and Figure 4.2). On the other hand, the costs of dealing with spoil on the reclamation/remediation projects can be a very high proportion of the total project cost (30-80% in the cases in this survey).

Table 4.3 Relative costs associated with surplus spoil from the projects

Project type and reference number	Unit cost for disposal, reuse and recycling of surplus spoil (£/m³)	Total costs for disposal, reuse and recycling of surplus spoil (£000)	Project cost (£M)	Surplus spoil costs as % of project cost
Road projects				
1	3.7	92	35	0.3
3	1.7	275	110	0.2
4	8.5	4000	80	5.0
9	1.3	742	245	0.3
10	0.4	230	39	0.6
14	10.6	1300	25	5.4
15	1.7	1700	80	2.0
21	5.5	1000	32	3.0
26	-	NA	30	-
31	-	NA	50	-
Site remediation projects				
2	-	2500	NA	-
5	33.0	480	1.4	34
7	2.5	6	3.7	0.2
17	4.8	663	1.4	46
22	-	NA	1.3	-
23	11.5	2300	7.5	31
28	10.0	4000	10	40
32	22.0	550	1.3	42
34	3.0	9000	11.5	78
35	36.6	6600	10.5	69
Power station				
24	20	3700	250	1.4
Quarry and landfill construction				
6	0.3	30	4	0.8
8	3.4	76	15	0.5
Commercial developments				
11	1.5	218	24	0.9
12	-	NA	10	-
Wastewater/water treatment plant				
13	-	NA	18	-
18	1.7	420	30	1.4
19	2.4	356	25	1.4
Pipeline				
16	-	NA	12.3	-
Dredging				
33	-	NA	0.4	-
Tunnels				
30	-	NA	NA	-
20	25	2300	57	4

NA: Not available

The unit costs of dealing with the surplus spoil in volume terms appear to range from as little as £0.5/m³ to as much as £23/m³ (see Figure 4.3).

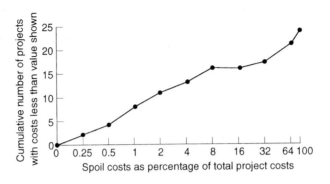

Figure 4.2 Distribution of spoil costs as proportion of the total project cost

Typical gate costs for disposal of spoil to landfill were between £10 and £15/m^3, but see Case Study 1 (Section 5.1) for which a considerable amount was disposed to landfill either free or for less than £3/m^3. The transport cost of removing the surplus spoil was not reported.

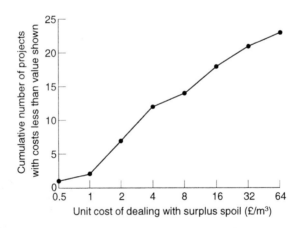

Figure 4.3 Distribution of unit costs for dealing with spoil in the projects

4.8 ## ROLES OF DIFFERENT PARTIES IN RELATION TO GROUND ENGINEERING WASTE

The survey shows that the contractor continues to have the greatest responsibility for the disposal of spoil on most projects. Some engineers and clients, however, were also involved in identification of the reuse and recycling options (Table 4.4).

Table 4.4 Parties involved in deciding the disposal, reuse and recycling options for spoil

	Numbers of projects		
Project types	**Client**	**Engineer**	**Contractor**
Roads	2	3	10
Site remediation projects	4	4	10
Power station	0	1	1
Commercial developments	0	2	2
Wastewater and water treatment plants	0	2	3
Quarry and landfill constructions	0	2	2
Tunnels	0	0	1
Dredging	1	1	1
Pipeline	0	0	1
Total	7	15	31

In most of the projects where the surplus spoil was reused, there was consideration at the design stage about how to maximise reuse and about the stockpiling arrangements that would be needed (Table 4.5). To some extent this would have been a function of the type of project and the need for spoil management, i.e. depending on the amount of surplus and how it would impinge on the project cost and programme.

Interestingly, none of the four projects which took part in spoil exchange had considered this at the planning stage.

Table 4.5 Consideration of spoil at design stage of the projects

	Replies as to whether the following matters were considered at the design stage of the project:								
Project types	**to maximise reuse of spoil?**			**to set aside area to stockpile spoil?**			**to participate in a spoil exchange scheme?**		
	Yes	**No**	**NA**	**Yes**	**No**	**NA**	**Yes**	**No**	**NA**
Roads	3	2	4	2	3	4	0	5	4
Site remediation projects	8	1	1	8	1	1	1	8	1
Power station	0	0	1	0	0	1	0	0	1
Quarry and landfill constructions	2	0	0	2	0	0	0	2	0
Commercial developments	0	2	0	0	2	0	0	2	0
Wastewater and water treatment plants	2	0	1	2	0	1	0	2	1
Tunnels	0	0	1	0	0	1	0	0	1
Dredging	1	0	0	1	0	0	0	1	0
Pipeline	0	1	0	0	1	0	0	1	0
Total	16	6	8	15	7	8	1	21	8

NA: Not available

4.9 LESSONS FOR SUBSEQUENT SURVEYS

The response rate to the questionnaire survey was high, although it was not an easy task to provide the requested information. There was a willingness to help provide answers, but many found difficulty in doing this because information about the disposal, reuse and recycling of spoil was not always readily available.

As much of the ground engineering works – and other operations that generate surplus materials – are carried out by subcontractors, any further survey should include subcontractors involved in the project. This will allow details such as haulage cost to be identified.

The questionnaire design could have been better, with clearer distinction between spoil, surplus spoil and waste: perhaps better still it should have used structured interviews, although this would have required more resources.

The subjects of the questionnaire survey and case studies (except the one in the planning stage) are all prior to introduction of the landfill tax on 1 October 1996. During the course of the survey, it became clear that the tax was having a considerable effect on the management of spoil and on efforts to minimise or reuse surplus spoil. It will be instructive to make a survey in a year or so in order to assess the effect of the tax on this sector of industry.

5 Case studies

This section describes six construction projects in relation to the generation of spoil and ways of dealing with surplus spoil. One is a project in the design stage so the description is about the estimation of quantities and the identification of options. The other five are either recently completed or still current projects. The scope they represent is wide, i.e.

1.   Construction of a new road (Section 5.1)

2.   A new wastewater tunnel (Section 5.2)

3.   Earthworks for a new power plant (Section 5.3)

4.   Canal dredging (Section 5.4)

5.   A contaminated site reclamation (Section 5.5)

6.   An infrastructure project (Section 5.6)

Information about each site was gained first through questionnaire replies from the project's client, designer and contractor and, later by follow-up interviews with key staff.

Drafts of these sections were sent for their comments and approval to the relevant parties in these projects. Although some of the information about these projects is already in the public domain, they and the organisations and places are not named.

Insofar as it possible to do so, each study follows the same pattern.

5.1 CASE STUDY 1: ROAD PROJECT

5.1.1 The project

The project is the on-line dualling of a main road in an urban area of the West Midlands of England. As well as construction of a dual carriageway where before there was a single-lane road, there are several associated footbridges and retaining walls to be built and part of the new road is to be in top-down constructed tunnel. The site is 2 km long. The project duration is three years and its total cost is £21 millions. Work started in April 1995, and was ongoing at the time of the survey.

5.1.2 The ground engineering operations and their scale

The ground engineering operations of the project include topsoil stripping, cut-and-fill earthworks, fill to structures, bored piling, and top-down tunnel construction. The bored piling is to create the side walls and central piers supporting the roof slab for the top-down constructed tunnel. The total cost of all these operations is about £1.9 million within a £21 million main works contract.

5.1.3 The ground materials and geological setting

The solid geology underlying the western 400 m of the route is a sequence of the Upper Coal Measures (mudstones, siltstones and occasional sandstones). In the central section of about 800 m are the mainly weak to moderately strong sandstones of the Sherwood Sandstone Group (Triassic), which at outcrop form an escarpment. Further east, the last 700 m of the new road are underlain by beds of the Mercia Mudstone Group, i.e. interbedded red-brown and green mudstones, siltstones and less frequent sandstones.

The drift is represented by firm and stiff glacial tills and some localised thin alluvial deposits. The surface consists of made ground, typically 1.5 m thick, but nearly 4 m in places, represented by colliery and pottery spoil, building rubble and ash.

5.1.4 The nature, amount and rate of spoil arising

The total excavated volume of ground materials is expected to be about 222 000 m^3, comprising: topsoil, stiff clay, sand and gravel, soft rock, and mixed materials. The total amounts of excavation are as shown below; values in Table 5.1 are those at September 1996:

- for roadworks, 174 000 m^3
- for structures, 29 000 m^3
- in arisings from the bored piling, structural excavations and drainage, 19 000 m^3

The excavation methods were auger boring for the bored piling of the walls forming the approach and top-down tunnel and backacter for the general earthworks and tunnelling (see Figure 5.1). Table 5.1 show the maximum rates of spoil generation.

Table 5.1 The volumes, nature and forms of excavated materials from the different types of ground engineering operations

Operation	Total quantity at Sept.1996 (m^3)	Excavated materials	Maximum rate of spoil production (m^3/day)
Topsoil stripping	Included below	Topsoil	114
Bored piling	11 000	Sand and gravel, weak sandstones	80
Cut-and-fill earthworks	101 000	Made ground, clays, sand and gravel	1000
Excavation for structures including tunnelling	15 000	Made ground, clay, sand and gravel, mudstone, marl, weak sandstone	1000

5.1.5   Disposal routes

Excavated materials where suitable are being used by the Contractor in the permanent works, but as the site is in an urban environment and much of the road is in cut, there is an excess of cut over fill, with little opportunity for reusing the excavated material in ancillary works. Thus a substantial proportion of the spoil has been and will be sent to landfill (see Table 5.2). The destinations for the spoil so far are as follows:

- 16 000 m^3 used in bulk earthworks

- 92 000 m^3 of earthworks excavation disposed off site to eleven landfill sites

- 15 000 m^3 of excavation for structures disposed off site to six landfill sites.

The expected destinations of the spoil still to be excavated are:

- 2000 m^3 to be used as selected fill to structures on site

- 14 000 m^3 to be used in bulk earthworks on the site

- 80 000 m^3 of further excavation to be disposed off site.

Of the off-site destinations for the spoil so far:

- 30 000 m^3 was reused as capping at four of the landfills, and was provided free of charge to those landfill sites

- 66 000 m^3 was disposed off site to eight other landfills, with charges ranging from £2/m to £16/m^3

- 1000 m^3 was reused off site on other construction sites for landscaping, about half of which was donated to the community and half sold to another contractor at a price of £2/m^3.

Figure 5.1   Case study 5.1
(a) earthworks at tunnel portal
(b) preparation of formation

Table 5.2 Destinations of the excavated materials

Source of spoil	Proportion (%) of excavated material to:	
	Landfill	Reuse
Bored piling	100	0
Cut and fill earth work	83	17
Excavation for structures	83	17
Topsoil stripping	0	100

5.1.6   Environmental impact of the spoil

Those materials excavated from the site which are mostly natural soils and rock were not expected to be contaminated. The made ground in the area of the site, however, could be contaminated in places and, indeed, the contract makes provision for use of the criteria of the Greater London Council (Kelly Table) for defining contaminated soils in dealing with surplus material. Analyses of samples of surplus materials, i.e. testing during the contract, showed concentrations of constituents such as sulphides, magnesium, manganese and hydrocarbons to be present in excavated materials such that they were considered by the local waste regulation authority to be U1A (Class B slight contamination or C contaminated) and U2 (Class D heavy contamination) under the Kelly Table criteria. An extract from the Kelly Table is given as Table 5.3. The hydrocarbons were expected to be present in the made ground and near-surface materials where there had been a garage and petrol station. Some of the sources of contamination in made ground and underlying soils are past and present industrial activities, human habitation, transport, etc. The level of contamination tends to decrease with depth and laterally with increasing distance from the sources.

In natural soils and rock, and in particular at greater depths, high concentrations of certain elements such as manganese, magnesium and sulphur as sulphides have been noted. These can be attributed to the natural processes of weathering and concentration which occured as a result of climatic changes, fluctuation of ground water levels or changes in the drainage pattern. The concentration of manganese (Mn) can be linked with the weathering of the surrounding sandstones of the Sherwood Sandstone Group, The sources of magnesium (Mg) can be linked with the slightly dolomitic matrix (Ca, $Mg(CO_3)_2$) of the siltstones and mudstones of the Mercia Mudstone Group. The concentrations of sulphides are noted in the glacial tills which are rich in fragments of coal and black shale, both containing pyrite (FeS_2) which is the most widespread sulphide mineral.

It is a matter of concern to the Client, Engineer and Contractor alike that the classification of waste materials is determined by the natural constituents of the soil which may also be present in the ground surrounding the works and even at the landfill site itself

Table 5.3 Extract from the definitions of contaminated soils used by Greater London Council

Parameter	Typical values for uncontaminted soils	Slight contamination	Contaminated	Heavy Contamination	Unusually heavy contamination
	Class A	Class B	Class C	Class D	Class E
SOIL CLASSIFICATION	U1	U1A	U1A	U2	U2
Manganese	0-500	500-1000	1000-2000	2000-1.0%	1.0%
Magnesium	0-500	500-1000	1000-2000	2000-1.0%	1.0%

Reference 56

5.1.7 Planning of the project and disposal of spoil

At the planning stage of the project, the Client carried out a feasibility study which comprised three separate assessments. As well as traffic and financial assessments, the environmental impact of the finished road was examined. The results were presented as part of a report to seek permission from the Secretaries of State for Transport and the Environment. This environmental impact assessment, however, did not include the impacts from the construction phase, such as disposal and reuse of spoil. The consultation with the local community, other interested parties, and regulatory and government bodies did not consider these issues in detail, because the choice of disposal sites is left to the Contractor.

5.1.8 Design stage planning for reuse, recycling of waste

The Engineer's estimates of the quantity, nature and form of the spoil were included in the project specification (Figure 5.2). Both reuse and recycling were considered at the planning stage of the project, but the responsibility for and choice of the disposal and reuse options, such as locations of off-site landfills, was left to the Contractor. This was to allow the Contractor to identify and select the most economical reuse and disposal options.

At the design stage of the project, the Engineer carried out a site investigation to establish the types of soils underlying the site, but no chemical analyses were carried out, either to classify soils into U1, U2 classes, etc., or to determine contamination levels. The results of this investigation were presented to the local Waste Regulation Authority and discussion took place to identify possible tipping facilities for both normal soils and soils which were believed to be contaminated as a result of industrial activities. No detailed chemical analyses of the soil were requested by the Waste Regulation Authority at that time, neither was the possibility raised that the amounts of naturally occurring metals and chemicals in the soil could create difficulties in selecting suitable disposal sites.

5.1.9 Regulatory requirements

The Contractor applied for a licence both to move and dispose spoil off site. The local waste regulation authority provided advice to individual operators of landfills contacted by the Contractor as to whether their landfill operation (i.e. holding a specific landfill operation licence) could take the spoil generated from this project.

5.1.10 Construction stage planning for reuse, minimisation, recycling of excavated material

Disposal of the spoil

The contract arrangement of this project meant that the Contractor was responsible for finding suitable landfill sites for the excavated materials (Figure 5.2). A list of prospective landfills was obtained at tender stage of the project, assuming the spoil was inert, i.e. uncontaminated. When the landfill operators of these sites were approached by the Contractor, they were required to consult the local waste regulation authority about whether their landfill operation licences would allow them to take the spoil. The authority then asked the Contractor to carry out chemical analyses on samples of the spoil. Classification of the spoil on the basis of these analyses according to criteria set by the contract (Greater London Council Kelly Table) (Table 5.3) put the spoil into soil classifications U1A and U2. As a result, the Contractor had to re-design the spoil disposal strategy.

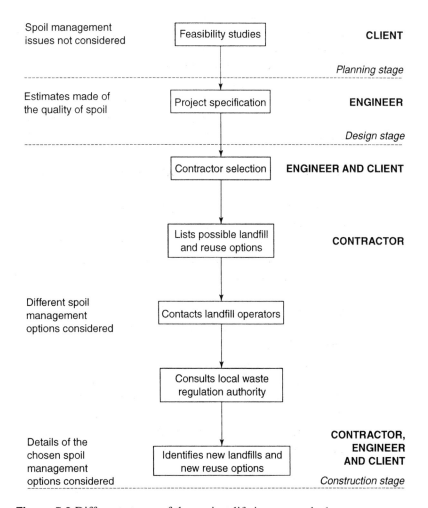

Spoil management
issues not considered   [Feasibility studies]   **CLIENT**

Planning stage

Estimates made of
the quality of spoil   [Project specification]   **ENGINEER**

Design stage

[Contractor selection]   **ENGINEER AND CLIENT**

[Lists possible landfill and reuse options]   **CONTRACTOR**

Different spoil
management
options considered   [Contacts landfill operators]

[Consults local waste regulation authority]

Details of the
chosen spoil
management
options considered   [Identifies new landfills and new reuse options]   **CONTRACTOR, ENGINEER AND CLIENT**

Construction stage

Figure 5.2 Different stages of the project life in case study 1

The eleven landfills that were used were all within 30 miles (as the crow flies), but five were within 10 miles and three, those taking the U2 waste, were between 20 and 30 miles from the site. The gate costs at some landfills were high because of the disposal of large quantities of spoil from adjacent contracts. The gate costs per m^3 were zero (at the four landfills where the material was provided as capping), between £1.00 and £2.44 at four sites (assumed to be for the Class B material), and £7.30 (assumed to be for the Class C material), £13.16, and £16.00 at the other two sites (for the U2, Class D waste).

The time to carry out the testing, to identify new landfill sites and to renegotiate with the landfill operators has considerably delayed the project. The testing of the spoil materials alone has cost some £50 000. Together with the landfill tax introduced in October 1996, the increased cost to the Client attributable to these aspects of dealing with the ground engineering spoil is likely to be of the order of £1 million.

Reuse options

The Contractor has tried to reduce net costs by maximising reuse of excavated material (on and off site). For example, as there is virtually no opportunity to reuse the spoil on site, e.g. in landscaping, other than in the designed permanent works, the Contractor has given away and sold some of the spoil to other projects (Table 5.2).

The cost involved in the reuse and recycling of the spoil was very small in this project. Most of the spoil generated was either directly reused or taken to landfills off site immediately after excavation. The only material that was temporarily stockpiled on the site was 5000 m³ of hard material from the demolition of the original road. This hard material was subsequently crushed and reused to lay haul roads for lorries. No cost was involved in the management and rental of the space for the stockpile.

5.1.11 Interactions between temporary and permanent works and excavated materials

The Engineer for the project was responsible for designing the permanent works where most of the spoil was generated and where a proportion was reused. Therefore the amount of spoil was estimated early in the project life (i.e. during the preparation of the project specification). The Contractor designed the temporary works such as traffic diversion roads. Thus it was only when the excavated materials were classified by the waste regulation authority to be U1A and U2 that the original plan for disposal had to be redesigned. While this change did affect the logistics in degree and amount, the methods were essentially unchanged, in that the spoil was taken to landfills in lorries, but with the requirement for additional precautions to seal against spillage and dust.

5.1.12 Lessons from the case study for the disposal, reuse and recycling of excavated materials

There are three ways that might bring significant savings of time and cost to a similar project.

1. To carry out at the site investigation stage chemical analyses of all anticipated surplus materials in accordance with the classification used by the local waste regulation authority.

2. To compare the results of these analyses with the criteria of the Environment Agency's *Interim guidance on the disposal of contaminated soils*. Thus the Client and Engineer would then be aware at an early stage of the project life that the spoil could be contaminated. This would allow suitable landfills to be identified more efficiently and cost-effectively. There is also a need to check the rate (m³/day) at which a landfill can accept material.

3. If the site is suitable and the Client has sufficient reason to do so, the Client could set up or purchase a landfill for the disposal of spoil.

A more general question is that of the classification of wastes where the criteria used are not necessarily indicators of contamination, but of a naturally present material. This is a question that should not just be asked at the investigation stage, but insofar as it is possible to do so, resolved with the waste regulators, so that the project costs can be maintained within the originally allowed budget.

5.2　CASE STUDY 2: TUNNELLING PROJECT

5.2.1　The project

The project was part of a major £500-million coastal water quality improvement scheme in the North West of England. The work involved construction of an 11.8 km interceptor tunnel (2.9 m diameter) to collect and transfer sewage from three catchment areas of two towns (with a total population of 350 000) to a wastewater treatment plant. The project duration was 27 months (work began in February 1994 and finished in May 1996). The total project cost was £75 million.

5.2.2　The ground engineering operations and their scale

Tunnelling in soft ground was the principal ground engineering operation. This was carried out by earth-pressure balance TBMs (tunnel boring machines) which advanced at up to 50 m a day. The cost of the tunnelling operation was £57 million (i.e. 76 % of the total project cost).

5.2.3　The ground materials and geological setting

The tunnel route extends along the coast with working and operational shafts at intervals in a popular seaside resort. The tunnel leads westwards to the treatment works site which is on a former river estuary flood plain, but has been used as a disposal area for domestic and agricultural waste and power station ash. The solid geology of relevance to the tunnelling is represented by three main strata which are bedded and folded (Figure 5.3). These are:

Upper Boulder Clay. This is a highly plastic, soft to firm glacial clay which in some areas includes laminated clays within it. There are also pockets of sand and gravel.

Middle sand. This comprises fine to coarse sand. Here also there are large lenses of soft laminated clays.

Lower Boulder Clay: This is a hard glacial clay with many erratic boulders derived from both igneous rocks and strong sedimentary rocks. There are also large pockets of silts, sands and coarse granular deposits, all under a hydrostatic head of up to 40 m.

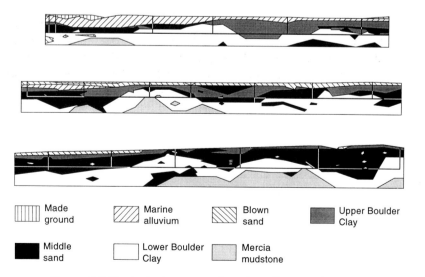

Figure 5.3 Geological cross section along the tunnel route

5.2.4   The nature amount and rate of spoil arising

The total volume of ground excavated was 92 000 m^3 comprising stiff clay, soft clay, sand and gravel (Table 5.4). Much of the spoil generated in this project was wet, the tunnel being below the water table and in heterogeneous materials. Thus it varied considerably in form as it was brought to the surface for disposal (Figure 5.4).

Table 5.4 The volumes, nature and forms of excavated materials from the ground engineering operation

Excavated materials	Total quantity (m^3)	Percentage (%)	Maximum rate of spoil production (m^3/day)
Stiff clay	23 000	25	64
Soft clay	32 200	35	90
Sand	23 000	25	64
Gravel	13 800	15	38
Total	92 000	100	-

Figure 5.4 Photograph of spoil generated in case study 2

5.2.5 Disposal routes

As reuse opportunities were limited on site, all excavated materials from the project were exported off site by lorries. The destinations of the spoil were as follows.

64 400 m³ (i.e. 70% of the total volume) comprising 100 % of the sand and gravel, and 50% of the stiff and soft clays excavated was reused off site (Table 5.5). This involved two nearby projects:

1. The main wastewater treatment plant (situated 500 m away from one end of the tunnel). Here, 27 600 m³ of the spoil were used as landscaping.

2. On 5 ha of land owned by the local council and 3 ha of farmland under private ownership, both adjacent to the tunnel work-sites, 36 800 m³ of the spoil were reused for capping and restoration.

27 600 m³ (i.e. 30 % of the total volume of spoil) was sent to a licensed landfill owned by the local county council, 300 m away from a work-site.

Table 5.5 Destinations of the excavated materials

Spoil type	Sand and gravel		Clay		
Destinations of the spoil	Quantity (m³)	Proportion (%) of spoil to:	Quantity (m³)	Proportion (%)of spoil to:	Total volume of spoil (m³)
Reuse off site					
– with treatment	18 400	50	0	0	18 400
– without treatment	18 400	50	27 600	50	46 000
Reuse on site	0	0	0	0	0
Landfill	0	0	27 600	50	27 600
Total	36 800	100	55 200	100	92 000

5.2.6 Environmental impact of the spoil

A site investigation was carried out at the design stage of the project. This involved sinking boreholes at spacings typically at 100 m centres, but sometimes much closer. The results of the chemical analysis showed that the site was not contaminated.

In so important and large a tunnelling scheme, particularly in an environmentally sensitive area with high public exposure in a holiday resort, the disposal of the spoil was recognised to be a major concern.

5.2.7 Planning of the project and disposal of spoil

A feasibility study was carried out at the planning stage. The study focused on the financial implications and the need for the project. The disposal, recycling and reuse of spoil were not specifically considered. It was planned that these issues should be dealt with by the contractor.

5.2.8 Design stage of planning for reuse, recycling of spoil

At the beginning of the project, the Client was responsible for the design of the tunnel. Later, this was transferred to an engineering company acting in an overall role to provide teams for the design, project and construction management for the scheme as a whole. Working in close collaboration with the project management team, the designer was able to incorporate details of the disposal, reuse and recycling of excavated materials into the design of the project (Figure 5.5).

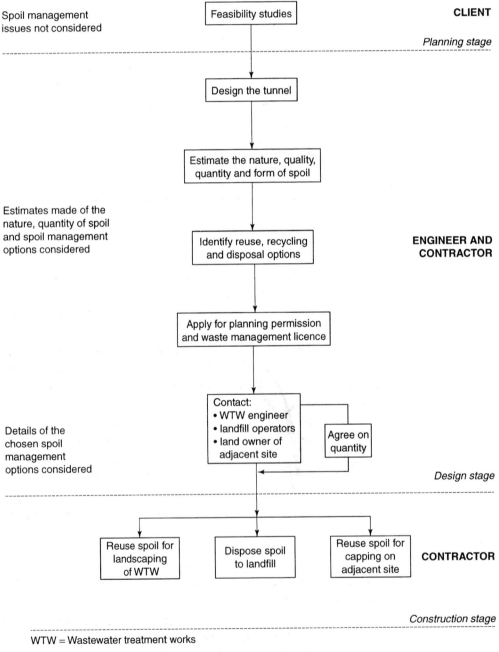

WTW = Wastewater treatment works

Figure 5.5 Different stages of the project life in case study 2

5.2.9   Regulatory requirements

The Client had applied for planning permission for the tunnel separately from that for the wastewater treatment scheme. On the site where the spoil was used as capping and the end use had not been designated (i.e. the site which was under private ownership), a Waste Management Licence was required. No licence was needed for disposal on the other land, which was owned by the Client and planned to have a recreational use.

5.2.10   Construction stage planning for reuse, minimisation, recycling of excavated material

The project involved drilling a tunnel where spoil minimisation was difficult. As a result the Client spent a total of £2.3 millions on disposal, reuse and recycling of spoil in this project. Table 5.6 shows that handling, haulage and treatment of the spoil by the landfill operator and the sub-contractor were the most expensive items.

Table 5.6 Break down of the disposal cost

Party	Items charged	Total cost (£ million)	Proportion (%) of the total cost
Landfill operator	Gate cost	0.16	7
	Handling and treatment	0.64	28
Sub-contractor	Haulage and treatment	1.50	65
Total		2.30	100

Disposal of the spoil

Although the landfills, transport arrangement, landfill gate costs and other charges by the landfill operator were agreed before construction commenced, the final cost for disposal of spoil was higher than that anticipated in the planning stage. This was for the following reasons.

1. The water content of the spoil varied greatly because of the different strata excavated in the tunnel. As a result, there were problems in handling and finding space for drying the spoil. 20% more spoil was sent to the landfill than had been anticipated in the planning stage.

2. The Client had to pay the landfill operator £2.00 per tonne for taking the spoil to particular areas within the landfill to be dried before placement in the landfill cells. The drying was achieved by stockpiling allowing the material to drain before rehandling. This made up 80% of the total payment to the landfill operator (Table 5.6).

3. Renegotiation with the landfill operator was needed when the initial time period of agreed gate costs expired. This subsequently led to an increase of £1 per tonne.

Reuse options

A considerable amount of spoil was able to be reused off site in this project (i.e. 70 % of the total volume). This was because:

- the main wastewater treatment plant needed a considerable amount of fill for landscaping work. This demand was realised very early in the project because landscaping was one of the conditions for the plant's planning permission.

- construction of the plant commenced at more or less the same time as the tunnel.

- the plant and the land where the spoil could be used as capping were close to the site (i.e. within 300 m). Haulage costs, therefore, were minimal.

Although most of the spoil was wet, 66% of the reused materials were not treated, but 50% of the sand and gravel was dried before reuse (Table 5.6). This involved temporary stockpiling on site with no cost in terms of management and rental of space. The tunnelling sub-contractor, however, charged the Client, £0.5/tonne for the treatment of materials like the wet soft clay.

5.2.11 Interaction between temporary and permanent works and excavation material

As the nature, form and quantity of spoil, and methods of dealing with these materials were considered in the design stage, the construction of permanent and temporary works were able to proceed as planned. It was only when the forms of the spoil were found to be very variable that problems in handling and treatment emerged. Although this did not affect the original disposal and reuse plan, the Client had to renegotiate with the landfill operator about putting more spoil in the landfill (Figure 5.5). This subsequently increased the disposal costs for the Client.

5.2.12 Lessons from the case study for the disposal, reuse and recycling of excavated materials

This project benefited in terms of time and cost from consideration of disposal and reuse of the spoil early in the project life; the construction stage was able to proceed smoothly.

There are, however, several lessons:

1. At the planning stage of the project, the Engineer on behalf of the Client should examine the following issues.

    - options for the disposal, reuse and recycling of spoil.

    - procedures needed for these options.

2. A disposal plan for the excavated materials should be developed before the project commences.

3. Provisions should be made in order that the chosen disposal, reuse and recycling options, and handing arrangements, can cope with unexpected situations, e.g. if the form of the spoil is more variable than anticipated in the design stage.

4. Drying wet spoil can be very expensive.

5. A local and national spoil exchange scheme could help the identification of reuse opportunities for the excavated materials.

5.3 CASE STUDY 3: POWER STATION

5.3.1 The project

This case study is about part of the civil engineering works for construction of a £250-million combined cycle power station in the Midlands. The contract was a turn-key one between the Client and the Main Contractor who also designed the power plant. The civil works were under a subcontract. The civil works began in November 1992 with clearance of the east part of the site and finished in November 1995.

5.3.2 The ground engineering operations and their scale

The ground engineering operations included bored piling, bulk excavation earthworks, and foundation and trench excavation (Table 5.7). They took place over periods ranging from 3 to 24 months. Virtually all the spoil generated in these works was surplus and taken to landfill. Their total cost was about £6 million, i.e. 6.4% of the total project cost.

Table 5.7 Duration and number of repeated ground engineering operations

Operations	Duration of work on site (months)	Number of separate operations	
Bored piling	3	700	(piles)
Bulk excavation	14.5	2	
Foundation excavation	12	40	
Trench excavation	24	Continuous	

5.3.3 The ground materials and geological setting

The site, previously that of a coal-fired power station, covers 219 acres and is split into two parts by a B-class road. The western boundary is a river; and a railway forms the eastern one. The west part of the site, the location of the former power station, is covered with made ground over alluvial sand and gravel near the river. The east part of the site, also with a surface of made ground, had been used for the storage of coal stocks and pulverised fuel ash (PFA), and held licensed plant for asbestos storage and handling. The whole site is underlain by Oxford clay. There is a perched water table associated with the river gravel in the area.

5.3.4 The nature, amount and rate of spoil arising

The total volume of spoil generated was 181 200 m^3 comprising clay (soft and stiff), sand and gravel. Table 5.8 shows the approximate quantities of the different types and forms of excavated material. About 95% of the spoil was surplus to site requirements for fill material.

Much of the surface material was found to be contaminated with asbestos (see Figure 5.6) and other remnant matter from the past use of the site. While desk studies had identified past usage of the site, it was after the start of site clearance works that the full extent of the contamination came to light. This was partly the result of the civil works contractor's commissioning a contamination survey for health and safety purposes and later as, at the request of the waste regulation authority, 120 probings were made across the eastern part of the site to classify the soils for waste disposal purposes. Initially the objective of the analyses on samples from probings was in terms of metal concentrations, particularly arsenic. It was finding asbestos in these samples that caused a major change in the nature of the excavation and disposal operations.

Management of the process of dealing safely and thoroughly with the asbestos on the site involved formal procedures on investigation, classification, excavation and disposal.

Table 5.8 Type, volume and rate of spoil excavation

Operations	Type of spoil	Quantity (m³)	Rate (m³/day)	Excavation method
Bored piling	Stiff clay	2000	50	Auger boring
	Sand and gravel	200	25	Auger boring
Bulk excavation earthworks	Made ground	93 000	1200	Backacter
	Soft clay	15 000	500	Backacter
	Stiff clay	7100	1200	Backacter
Foundation excavation	Sand and gravel	7600	200	Backacter
	Stiff clay	48 600	250	Backacter
Trench excavation	Sand and gravel	1600	50	Backacter
	Stiff clay	6100	300	Backacter

Figure 5.6 Bags of asbestos revealed during bulk excavation

5.3.5 Disposal routes

The destinations for the spoil were as follows:

- 78 100 m^3 (i.e. 43 % of the volume of spoil) to a field south of the site for disposal in a specially created landfill.

- 93 000 m^3 (i.e. 51.5 % of the volume of spoil) which was classed as either Special or Difficult Waste was taken to a licensed landfill 37 km away with a gate cost of £37.5/m^3.

- 10 100 m^3 (i.e. 5.5 % of the volume of spoil) was used for backfill to new structures of the new power station.

Thus nearly 95% of the spoil was disposed off site to landfill, for the following reasons:

- very little fill was needed for the new works

- the site area was too fully occupied by the new construction to give any opportunity for mitigation fills, such as landscaping

- there was no readily suitable uses for the clay spoil, e.g. on other construction sites

- most of the materials from the bulk excavation were contaminated by asbestos. They were classified as Special Waste (Category E) and Difficult Waste (Category D) by the local waste regulation authority. As such, these materials could only be disposed of at designated landfills.

5.3.6 Environmental impact of the spoil

Both parts of the site included areas that had been used for storage, i.e. of coal, PFA and asbestos, with resulting contamination of the ground by:

- PAHs, toluene extract, etc. from the coal stockyard

- heavy metals such as zinc, copper, nickel and arsenic, from PFA

- asbestos as crocidolite and in other forms

- increased sulphate contents

- PCBs, mineral oils and toxic metals.

Although the concentrations of metals were in many instances above the ICRCL threshold levels (see Table 5.9), it was the presence of asbestos that led to the classification of spoil as Difficult or Special Waste by the local waste regulation authority. The areas of asbestos are marked on Figure 5.7. The waste classification was on the following basis:

- Difficult Waste, Category D: spoil containing less than 1% by weight of free fibre of asbestos types other than crocidolite

- Special Waste, Category E: spoil containing crocidolite or more than 1% by weight of free fibre of other types of asbestos.

5.3.7 Planning of the project and disposal of spoil

At the planning stage of the project, a number of studies which focused on the following issues were carried out.

- need for the power plant

- reasons for building the power plant on the site

- financial implications

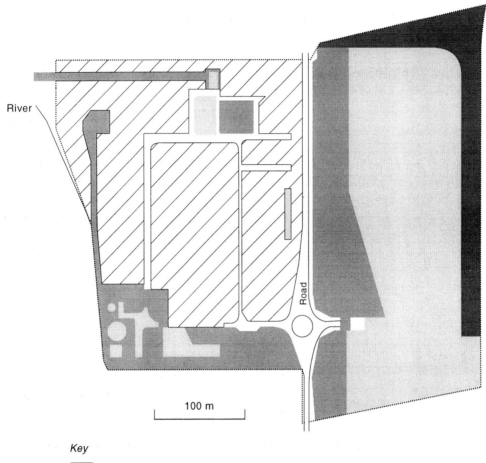

River

Road

100 m

Key

■ Extensive asbestos contamination covered by a clay capping

▨ Areas where contaminated material was removed and backfilled with clean clay

□ Areas where contaminated material was removed to natural clay

⧄ Full extent of contamination not proven. Information suggests low level of asbestos, metal and organic contamination. Covered by 300 mm of topsoil

······· Site boundary

Figure 5.7 Area of the site contaminated by asbestos

Table 5.9 Results of the site investigations

Metals	Number out of the 110 probings in which metal concentrations were above the ICRCL threshold level
Zinc	3
Copper	9
Arsenic	23
Boron	10
Nickel	1
Selenium	2

The Client also submitted an application in 1991 to the Department of Trade and Industry for the power station under Section 36 of the Electricity Act 1989. Although an environmental assessment was made, there was no special consideration of spoil disposal, reuse or recycling.

It appears that appraisal of the ground conditions at the site in respect of spoil and its disposal was limited to desk study.

5.3.8   Design stage of planning for reuse, recycling of spoil

The design stage of the project included estimates of the cut-and-fill balance and the quantity, nature and form of surplus spoil from the bulk excavations. Although the construction contract had started before the site investigation to provide information on ground contamination was carried out (Figure 5.8), the Turn-key Contractor was able to incorporate the following provisions into the work:

- health and safety measures provided by the Civil Contractor

- minimisation of the potential of the ground engineering operations to cause adverse off-site environmental impact

- appropriate classification of excavated materials to be disposed off site.

The Turn-key Contractor divided the site into different categories, depending on what was known about the asbestos contamination, i.e.:

- areas with no contamination

- areas where the asbestos was present in small amounts

- areas where the extent of asbestos concentration was unknown

- areas heavily contaminated by asbestos that should be left undisturbed after covering with a capping layer.

In the event that an excavation had to be made in an area of heavy asbestos contamination, the capping layer was fully reinstated thereafter. For example, on the embankment along the eastern boundary, there were bags of asbestos, some of which were broken, at depths from 1 to 2 m below the slope surface. Here the uppermost material was excavated to improve stability of the slope, the rest was left in place and capped by geotextile overlain by 1 m of clay and 0.25 m of topsoil.

In the planning and at the beginning of the design stage of the project, neither the Client nor the Turn-key Contractor were fully aware of the extent of the contamination, particularly the presence of asbestos. Consequently, there were delays that affected the handling and disposal of the spoil during the construction stage. As a result the total spoil disposal cost was greatly increased.

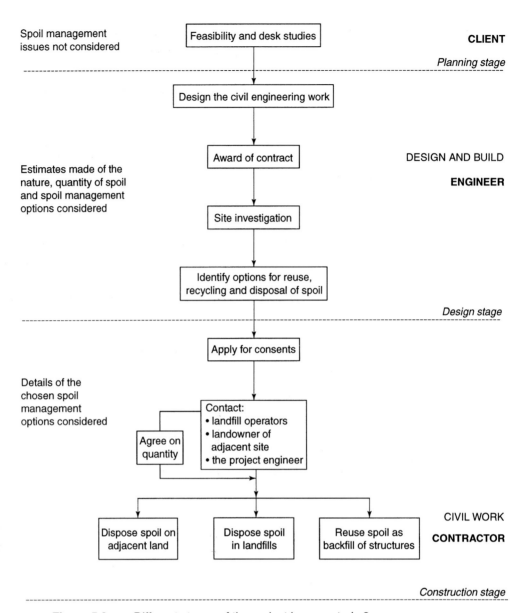

Figure 5.8 Different stages of the project in case study 3

5.3.9   Regulatory requirements

The Client was responsible for applying for consents that relate to the construction and operation of the power plant, such as planning permission. Although an environmental assessment was carried out and a number of conditions relating to environmental issues of the project were imposed with the planning permission, none of them was about the reuse, recycling or disposal of the spoil.

The Civil Works Contractor applied for planning permission and a waste disposal licence for disposing spoil to a field at the south of the site. The permission was conditional upon the deposited material being dry and inert and that it be placed in accordance with an approved scheme of landscaping. As the owner of this landfill, the Civil Works Contractor took on responsibility for monitoring the effect on ground conditions there and has paid a fee to the Environment Agency in order that they can check that the work was done satisfactorily. Waste Transfer Notes were also required by the local council to record the movement of lorries that carried contaminated spoil out of the site.

5.3.10   Construction stage planning for reuse, minimisation, recycling of excavated material

Samples of the spoil were taken and analysed throughout the construction stage of the project. Water samples taken from drains and outflows into the river were also monitored. The results were sent to the Turn-key Contractor who classified the material on the basis of criteria agreed with the local waste regulation authority. The Turn-key Contractor subsequently issued instruction to the Civil Works Contractor for the use or disposal of the spoil.

The Civil Contractor prepared a Method and Management Control Statement to govern the safe removal of contaminated material from the site after consultation with the Health and Safety Executive (HSE), the environmental health department in the local council, the waste regulation authority, the Highways Agency and the (then) NRA.

Heath and safety plans and statements were also prepared which include the following provisions:

- all personnel had to wear masks and protective clothing during operations which involved the excavation of contaminated materials
- a decontamination room was built with changing facilities for personnel
- vehicle washing and decontamination facilities were provided (Figure 5.9)
- all excavators engaged in the movement of contaminated spoil were supported by a bowser with a fully masked operator to damp down the digging face
- contaminated spoil was transported on and off site by covered and registered lorries. The Civil Works Contractor recorded the movement of lorries which carried the contaminated spoil out of the site. These vehicles had to be cleaned and sheeted before leaving the site
- water from wheel washing and temporary holding lagoons had to be removed from the site. Initially assumed to be special waste, it was taken by tanker off site to a designated treatment plant; later analyses showed it was not highly contaminated so that a different off-site disposal facility could be used
- the windows and cab doors of excavator and lorries were required to be closed during the excavation operations.

Staff of the environmental health department of the local authority and from HSE inspected the site regularly throughout the work.

The Civil Works Contractor had appointed environmental consultants to undertake regular monitoring for ground contamination and the on-site analysis of soil, water and airborne asbestos fibres throughout the excavation operations. They also assisted with supervision of the site workers in relation to contamination. This monitoring enabled remedial action to be put in place efficiently when the contamination risk was identified. The Client and the Turn-key Contractor employed their own environmental consultants.

Figure 5.9 Photograph showing wheel wash facility installed with operatives suitably clad for hose down

Disposal of the spoil

The Civil Works Contractor consulted both the Turn-key Contractor and Client before disposing excavated material off site. Although for inert spoil, the availability and proximity of the field owned by the Contractor for disposal was convenient with low haulage costs, there were, however, problems in the construction stage that led to increased total disposal costs for the spoil.

1.   Changes in legislation during the construction stage meant that the Civil Works Contractor had to continue to monitor the condition of the field disposal site after the contract had finished. This cost the Contractor a total of £370 000.

2.   Few landfills in the local area could take spoil contaminated by asbestos, a weak position for negotiating the gate cost with the landfill operators concerned. As a result the disposal of contaminated spoil was much higher than the inert materials, i.e. from £2.75/m^3 at the landscaping site to £13/m^3 and, for the most contaminated material, £37.5/m^3 (Table 5.10). The cost to the Client for disposal of spoil containing asbestos was of the order of £5 million.

Reuse of spoil

The Civil Works Contractor tried to reuse the spoil where possible, but there were few opportunities in the scheme design and the asbestos and metals contamination almost completely precluded other uses. As a result, only 5.6% of the spoil (i.e. 10 100 m^3) was reused. All of this was temporarily stockpiled to remove water before its use as backfill for structures. It was estimated that the cost for management of the stockpile was about £0.50/m^3, small compared with the inert disposal cost (Tables 5.10 and 5.11).

Table 5.10 Disposal cost for the spoil

Operation	Type of spoil	Gate cost (£/m^3)	Distance (km)	Total cost (£)
Bored piling	Stiff clay	2.75	1	5500
	Sand and gravel	2.75	0.5	415
Bulk excavation earthworks	Soft clay	13.0	20	195 000
	Mixed material	37.5	37	3 480 000
Foundation excavation	Stiff clay	2.75	0.5	126 000
	Sand and gravel	2.75	0.5	19 700
Trench excavation	Stiff clay	2.75	0.5	16 800
	Sand and gravel	2.75	0.5	44 500
Total				£3.8 million

Table 5.11 Treatment cost of the spoil

Operation	Spoil reused	Volume (m^3)	Stockpile cost (£)	Unit stockpile cost (£/m^3)
Bulk excavation earthwork	Stiff clay	7100	3550	0.5
Foundation excavation	Stiff clay	2500	1500	0.6
	Sand and gravel	500	–	–
Total		10 100	5050	

5.3.11 Interactions between temporary and permanent works and excavated materials

The Turn-key Contractor was responsible for the permanent works – where most of the spoil was generated – and that section of site which was heavily contaminated by asbestos. The site investigation could only be carried out after work on site clearance had started and only then was there a clear indication of the nature, extent and degree of contamination. Thereafter the reuse and disposal of spoil were able to proceed as planned to the extent that the spoil could be classed as inert.

The Civil Works Contractor designed and constructed the temporary works. Insofar as these were on the western part of the site – where both the asbestos contamination and the excavation volumes were small and the arrangements for handling contaminated spoil were in place – disposal of the material was not a big problem.

Nevertheless construction was slowed down as an instruction from the Turn-key Contractor was needed each time contaminated spoil was found before the Civil Works Contractor could proceed with its disposal.

5.3.12 Lessons from the case study for the disposal, reuse and recycling of excavated materials

There are five general lessons for other similar projects.

1. The Client needs to ensure that records of land use and previous investigations are kept safe.

2. A design-and-build contractor needs to have a sound understanding of the contaminants present on a site before entering a contract or the contract should be set up with the flexibility to cope with the possibility of contamination and its consequences for the work. This could be done in two ways:

   - the nature and extent of contamination on site should be made known to the potential contractors at tender stage, e.g. by a Consultant appointed by the Client carrying out an initial desk study and then designing and supervising a comprehensive site investigation, before the tender documents for the main works are drawn up

   - if not, the contract should make provision to allow the appointed Turn-key Contractor to complete an investigation of agreed scope and to re-price relevant tasks in the light of the findings.

3. It is no longer possible, if it ever was, to derogate responsibility for waste, particularly when it may be contaminated. All the parties in the construction contract have to be involved in the processes that lead to successful management of the spoil, i.e. whether in obtaining planning permission, approval by waste and environmental regulators, or in satisfying local public concerns.

4. Monitoring the spoil may be essential for health and safety reasons.

5. Achieving a cut-and-fill balance, e.g. by design of 'extra' landscaping, in the design stage is increasingly important as the costs of landfill disposal rise.

5.4   CASE STUDY 4: DREDGING PROJECT

5.4.1   The project

The project is the dredging of a 2 km section of canal in the West Midlands of England (Figure 5.10). This is Phase IV of a water quality improvement scheme for the canal. The total cost of the project is £330 000. The work, programmed to last 20 weeks began in January 1997.

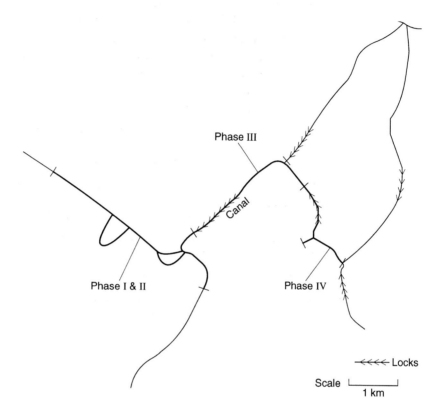

Figure 5.10 Map of the canal

5.4.2   The ground engineering operations and their scale

The ground engineering operation of the project is the dredging of contaminated sediment typically to a depth of 1.5 m below the water level. The cost of the operation is £300 000, i.e. nearly 90% of the project cost.

5.4.3   The ground materials and geological setting

Site investigation shows that sediment is 0.6 to 1.75 m below the water level. Fragments of bricks, concrete, glass, etc. are present on the surface of the sediment. The sediment is typically a wet black organic gravelly sandy silt with masonry rubble, scrap metal and glass. The sizes of materials present at various depths of the canal also differ greatly (Table 5.12).

5.4.4   The nature, amount and rate of spoil arising

The total volume of material excavated is expected to be about 6000 m^3 comprising silt, sand rubble, etc. (Figure 5.11). Table 5.13 shows the volume and nature of spoil generated at the time of preparing this report (i.e. the first three weeks after the project has begun). Optimum production is expected to rise to 400-500 m³ week. The excavation method is by dredging using backacters mounted on pontoons which load the dredged materials into barges.

Table 5.12 Size of different types materials present at different sections of the canal

depth of sample (m)	% coarse debris	% fine - medium gravel	% sand	% silt	% clay
1.70 – 2.20	<5	3	5	47	41
1.70 – 2.20	15	25	19	36	6
2.20 – 2.50	15	4	27	39	15
1.00 – 1.40	55	27	10	← 8 →	
1.70 – 1.90	55	29	12	← 4 →	
0.70 – 1.10	0	7	21	59	13
1.50 – 1.60	60	11	18	8	3
0.00 – 0.30	85	2	.1	10	2
1.20 – 1.40	0	16	12	67	5
1.40 – 1.70	40	29	24	← 6 →	
0.70 – 1.10	25	22	15	32	6
1.30 – 1.40	30	36	18	← 16 →	
1.00 – 1.30	23	45	22	← 9 →	
1.10 – 1.40	15	32	27	25	1

Note: clay to medium gravel fraction adjusted to take into account % of coarse debris estimated in the field sample.

Table 5.13 Volume and nature of the spoil in first 3 weeks of the project

Operations	Type of spoil	Quantity (m³)	Excavation method
Dredging	Mixed materials	600	Floating backacter

Figure 5.11   Photograph of spoil generated from case study 4

5.4.5　Disposal routes

The 6000 m^3 of spoil expected to be generated by the project will be put through a 40 mm screen. The estimated volumes and destination of the resulting materials will be as follows

- 4600 m^3 of wet sludge will be treated with lime and used to form intercell bunds in a daily cover in a landfill off site.

- 200 m^3 of spoil comprising metal, plastic and wood fragments will be sorted and recycled with the residue disposed to landfill off site.

- 1200 m^3 of masonry rubble will be washed, crushed and reused as granular fill and sold to a third party.

The sediments in the canal are contaminated by heavy metals, phytotoxic metals and hydrocarbons. A summary of the sediment analytical results compared with guidelines produced by the Dutch National Institute of Public Health and Environmental Protection [55] is given in Table 5.14. In the Netherlands, remedial action is necessary when intervention values are exceeded.

The results show high levels of toxic metals, cadmium and chromium as well as the phytotoxic metals, copper, nickel, and zinc are present in this sediment, with 43 – 93% of the analyses exceeding the Dutch Category C intervention values. These contaminants are released into the water column as boat traffic travels along the canal, disturbing the sediments. (Note that Category C is no longer used in the Netherlands).

5.4.6　Design stage of planning for reuse, recycling of spoil

Disposal, reuse and recycling of spoil make up more than 50% of the total cost of many urban waterway dredging projects in the UK. Thus the Engineer had to consider the physical and chemical nature of the arisings and to estimate the quantity of the spoil carefully in the design stage of the project. Furthermore, the Client here chose to treat the spoil before disposing it to landfill off site. Although the addition with quicklime has cost an extra £18 000 compared to direct disposal of wet dredgings, the Client believes that the benefits of the treatment outweigh its cost. This is because:

- The addition of lime can reduce the mobility of the heavy metals present in the spoil. This means that the materials will be considered by the local waste regulation authority as a lower disposal category.

- Reduction of the water content makes handling of the spoil easier.

- The dredged length of the canal and the cost involved in this project are small. The Client used this as a pilot study to assess the financial and environmental implications of lime. Trends in landfill disposal costs indicate rapidly rising prices for wet dredging disposal.

- The approach is consistent with the Client's image as a 'green' organisation.

Table 5.14 Summary of sediment analyses and comparision with Dutch guidelines[55]

Contaminent	Typical sediment concentration (mg/kg)	Dutch intervention value (mg/kg)
Arsenic	50 – 300	55
Cadmium	1 – 60	12
Chromium	60 – 4000	380
Copper	500 – 30 000	190
Nickel	100 – 2200	210
Lead	500 – 5000	530
Zinc	500 – 2500	720
Mineral oil	2 000 – 34 000	5000

5.4.7   Regulatory requirements

The Client used its General Development Order powers to set up the site. Planning permission was not necessary as dredging and spoil treatment was carried out within the curtilage of the canal. The Contractor's plant has been classified as exempt under the Waste Management Regulations. The Contractor completed a waste transfer treatment note for each load leaving the site.

5.4.8   Construction stage planning for reuse, minimisation, recycling of excavated material

Disposal of the spoil

Spoil when generated is fed into a mobile screening machine to remove large fragments of debris > 40 mm. Approximately 4600 m³ of the spoil comprising mostly silt and sand will be placed in a blending chamber together with approximately 10% lime. A discharge conveyor is used to transfer the mixture into a storage bin for transport to the landfill off site (Figure 5.12).

Although the disposal and reuse options were identified at the design stage, the landfill operator increased the gate cost by 100% two months before the project began. This means that the Client would have to pay an additional of £54 000 for disposing the spoil to the landfill.

Reuse of spoil

The Contractor has tried to maximise the reuse of spoil. The screening process should allow the Contractor to recycle 1200 m³ of washed rubble as granular fill.

Figure 5.12   Photograph showing screening and the treatment of spoil: case study 4

5.4.9   Interaction between temporary and permanent works and excavated materials

The Engineer is responsible for adequately describing the *in-situ* material and the anticipated volumes to be removed, as well as monitoring the part-dredged canal to ascertain that minimum navigable depths and acceptable residual contaminant levels are achieved.

The Contractor is responsible for the design of the dredging process. Disposal, reuse and recycling of the spoil were considered at the design stage, and options for spoil treatment invited as part of the tender process. The Contractor also prepared a method statement outlining how the spoil will be dealt with. There is very little reuse of spoil in the construction of temporary works.

5.4.10   Lessons from the case study for the disposal, reuse and recycling of excavated materials

There are a number of aspects which could benefit future projects.

- Addition of lime to wet spoil has a number of advantages:
  - it reduces the volume of spoil that needs to be disposed to landfill off site.
  - it immobilises heavy metals present in the spoil.
  - it makes the handling of spoil easier.
  - as a stabilised soil it may have enhanced engineering uses.

- Attention should be paid to matching the spoil generation rate to the processing rate of the lime addition plant.

- Reuse, recycling and disposal of spoil should be considered in the design and planning stages of the project.

- Heavy metals may be present in sediment, but are not necessarily a source of risk. It is often the case that the mobile contaminants have been dissolved or washed away, leaving immobile (and hence relatively harmless) chemicals. Tests of metal concentrations should be complemented by leaching tests to determine the mobility of the contaminants, as recommended by the Environment Agency.

5.5   CASE STUDY 5: RECLAMATION PROJECT

5.5.1   The project

The project was the reclamation works carried out on a 2.4 ha of contaminated site in the West Midlands of England. The work involved removal of contaminated soil, backfilling with clean granular fill, encapsulation and containment of heavily polluted area by slurry trench of areas where the made ground was deeper and saturated below about 1.5 m – which would have made excavation prohibitively expensive. Structural stabilisation and refurbishment of a canal wall, drainage and fencing works were also carried out. (Figure 5.13)

The total cost of the project was £1.25 million and the duration was 5 months (work began in March 1995 and finished in July 1995).

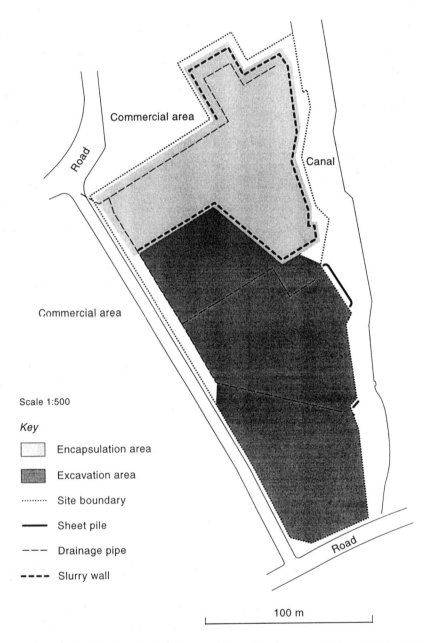

Figure 5.13 Plan showing different ground operations on the site in case study 5

5.5.2   The ground engineering operations and their scale

The ground engineering operations of the project were general excavation, installation of the slurry trench cut-off, cut-and fill earthworks and construction of a sheet pile wall. The cost of these operations was £1 million (90% of the total project cost).

Figure 5.14 View of part of the reclamation site

5.5.3   The ground materials and geological setting

The general strata of the site are as follows:

- Made ground

  This comprises concrete overlying a loose granular fill with ash, clinker, plastic and wire fragments, slag, concrete and brick structures and former foundations. Below is a layer of cohesive fill of sandy silts, old foundations, ash and clayey silty sand.

- Boulder clay

  This is a silty reddish brown firm to stiff gravelly clay with boulders and pockets of soft silty sandy clay.

- Clent Formation

  This comprises silty red brown fine to medium sandstone and some weak red brown mudstone.

5.5.4   The nature, amount and rate of spoil arising

The total volume of material excavated in the project was 24 000 m^3 comprising ash, clinker, rubble and clay from the made ground, concrete from foundations and earlier structures and infills from a former canal basin. Most of these materials were dry. The excavation was by swing shovel. 1200 m^3 of bricks, concrete blocks and slabs from demolition of former buildings were stockpiled on the site before the project began. (Table 5.15)

5.5.5 Disposal routes

The disposal routes for the spoil were as follows:

- 22 000 m^3 of excavated materials that were contaminated by heavy metals and PCBs were sent to landfill off site
- 2100 m^3 of masonry and concrete rubble and slabs from the demolition of former buildings and foundations on site which were crushed and screened. The clean coarse fraction was stockpiled on site and subsequently reused as backfill to excavations. (Figure 5.15)
- Crushed fines were used as a blinding layer prior to geomembranes placement.

Figure 5.15 Screened concrete and masonry stockpiles

Table 5.15 Volume of the spoil and the excavation methods

Operations	Quantity (m^3)	Excavation method
General excavation	21 000	Backacter
Slurry trench cut off	1000	Backacter
Demolition of former buildings	2100	Backacter's breaker

5.5.6 Environmental impact of the spoil

Considerable areas of the site were contaminated by heavy metals including arsenic, cadmium, zinc, etc. Polyaromatic hydrocarbons were also found. PCBs were present in some areas from coolant spills from transformers.

5.5.7 Planning of the project and disposal of spoil

The Client and Engineer had carried out a number of feasibility studies at the planning stage of the project. They had identified the need for crushing and screening of concrete and masonry so as that these materials could be reuse as an engineered backfill. Research into alternative methods of dealing with the spoil was curtailed by the availability of funds being time-limited.

5.5.8 Design stage planning for reuse, recycling of spoil

As this project aimed to reduce the risks arising from the site, the design and execution of the ground engineering operation depended on the extent and nature of contaminants present in the ground. For example, in areas where high levels of contaminants were found and the depth of these materials precluded economic excavation, a slurry trench cut-off wall and clay and geomembrane capping were installed to prevent migration of the contaminant.

The nature, quantity and form of spoil were estimated in the planning stage of the project. The Engineer had also identified the types of materials that could be used as backfill and capping layers in the project specification.

5.5.9 Regulatory requirements

Planning permission was applied for. Although this was a site remediation project, no conditions with the permission were imposed on the reuse, recycling and disposal of spoil.

5.5.10 Construction stage planning for minimisation, reuse, recycling of excavated material

Disposal of the spoil

As there were a number of landfills in the locality willing to take contaminated spoil generated from this project, the Contractor did not have significant problems in identifying suitable landfills.

The spoil was loaded by backacters straight into lorries which were then sheeted and sent direct to the landfill sites. A Waste Transfer Note was required for each load. The total cost for disposing the spoil, which included the gate cost, and haulage cost was £484 000 (i.e. approximately £23/m^3 at 1995 prices).

Reuse options

Demolition rubble and slabs were crushed and screened to be used as engineered backfill (Figure 5.16). This cost a total of £25 500 (i.e. £7.7/m^3 at 1995 prices).

At the construction stage, the Contractor offered an alternative clean material from another construction site to be used as the bulk backfill (i.e. a natural Permian-age sand of DOT Specification for Highway Works Class 1B) as opposed to the backfill class previously specified. The Engineer agreed to the use of this material because it was considered that its engineering properties would be suitable (see Figure 5.17). The use of this Class1B material reduced the estimated project cost by £30 000 (i.e.a saving of £2.0/m^3).

Figure 5.16 Screening recycled concrete and masonry in case study 5

5.5.11   Interactions between temporary and permanent works and excavated materials

Although the Engineer was responsible for design of the permanent works, the disposal and recycling options for the spoil were also determined at the design stage of the project. As the Contractor was readily able to identify a landfill site, the disposal of spoil was carried out as planned.

The Contractor's design and construction of temporary works involved only small quantities of spoil being generated.

5.5.12   Lessons from the case study for the reuse, recycling, and disposal of excavated materials

The Engineer had chosen excavation and off-site disposal as the way to remove hazards from the ground of the project site. The generation of a large quantity of spoil was therefore unavoidable, and the ways that the Client, the Engineer and the Contractor handled these materials became vital to the success of the project.

Aspects which might help similar projects in the future are:

- Early consideration of the management of spoil is vital to the efficiency of site remediation projects.

- Importation of clean spoil from other construction sites rather then quarries or similar aggregate suppliers could reduce the total project cost. A properly managed and organised local or national spoil exchange scheme would assist the Engineer and the Contractor to explore opportunities of reusing the spoil.

Figure 5.17 Sand backfill (DOT Class 1B)

5.6 CASE STUDY 6: INFRASTRUCTURE PROJECT

5.6.1 The project

The case study is a 15-km long transport infrastructure project, which is currently at design stage.

5.6.2 The ground engineering operations and their scale

The ground engineering operations considered are the earthworks and two cut-and-cover tunnel lengths. The cost of these operations has not been finalised, but is expected to be several tens of £ millions.

5.6.3 The ground materials and geological setting

The route crosses progressively older Cretaceous age rocks from north to south. The solid succession includes high plasticity clays, loams, silts and sandy clays, and calcareous sandstones and siltstones. The drift deposits are dominated by Head (solifluction deposits). Alluvium is present in river valleys.

5.6.4 The nature, amount and rate of spoil arising

The total volume of ground material to be excavated is estimated to have an *in-situ* volume of 1.6 million m^3 (approximately 2 million m^3 bulked) comprising:

- 6 % Stratum 1: Made Ground
- 20 % Stratum 2: Head
- 19 % Stratum 3: Sands
- 25 % Strata 4 and 5: High plasticity overconsolidated clays
- 15 % Stratum 6: Sands, silts and clays
- 15 % Stratum 7: Sands, calcareous sandstones and siltstones.

200 000 m^3 of the cut volume is a contingency allowance for 'dig out' of soft and potentially unstable materials mainly below embankment foundations. 45% of this is from beneath one long embankment.

5.6.5 Disposal routes

A number of disposal options for the spoil were examined. These were:

- reuse as 'structural' embankment fill and/or mitigation fill
- sale to third parties
- disposal to landfills off site. Spoil to be disposed of in this way would include:
  - contaminated materials
  - inert spoil comprising clay and other material which is unacceptable for structural and mitigation fills because of its high moisture content. The addition of a small dosage of lime is an option to render such spoil acceptable for reuse by drying it out, but this is not included here.

5.6.6   Environmental impact of the spoil

The Designer anticipates that approximately 55 000 m³ of contaminated spoil will be generated from two particular locations along the route. The bulk of this material is to be removed not because it is contaminated, but for topographical or engineering requirements. Risk assessments were made to evaluate each potentially contaminated site crossed or affected by the alignment. The following provisions have been made in the earthworks planning:

1. A contingency of 2 m depth of unclassified contaminated materials is assumed at one site where, as a result of a detailed desk study, these materials are suspected to be present. As a result of difficulty in gaining access to this site, the quantities and degree of contamination of these materials are still to be confirmed by site investigation.

2. A contingency of 1 m depth of special waste has been made for another location where asbestos was identified in the site investigation.

5.6.7   Planning of the project and management of spoil

The information in this case study shows how the project planning takes full account of the need for managing the bulk excavated materials to minimise waste.

The Designer had developed a bulk spoil management strategy for the project. This defines the hierarchy in which spoil should be dealt with as follows (most preferable solution first):

1. Acceptable excavated materials as defined by the DOT Specification for Highway Works to be used in engineered 'structural' embankment fills.

2. Acceptable excavated materials to be used in mitigation measures such as noise bunds, landscaping, etc.

3. Acceptable excavated materials to be made available to third parties.

4. Excavated materials to be disposed of:
   - on site
   - to local sites
   - to more distant sites within the route corridor.

5.6.8   Design stage of planning for management of spoil

The above strategy was used to produce earthworks movement diagrams and Figure 5.18 shows an example of part of one of these. A cut-and-fill balance for the spoil was also carried out (Table 5.16).

This balance is a conservative estimate and assumes the following:
- that there will be no lime and/or cement processing of any spoil materials
- that the less contaminated (non hazardous) portion of the contaminated spoil can be used for mitigation fill provided that it is not placed near to building or civil engineering structures or on flood plains or near watercourses.

Volumes in m³ × 10³ of:

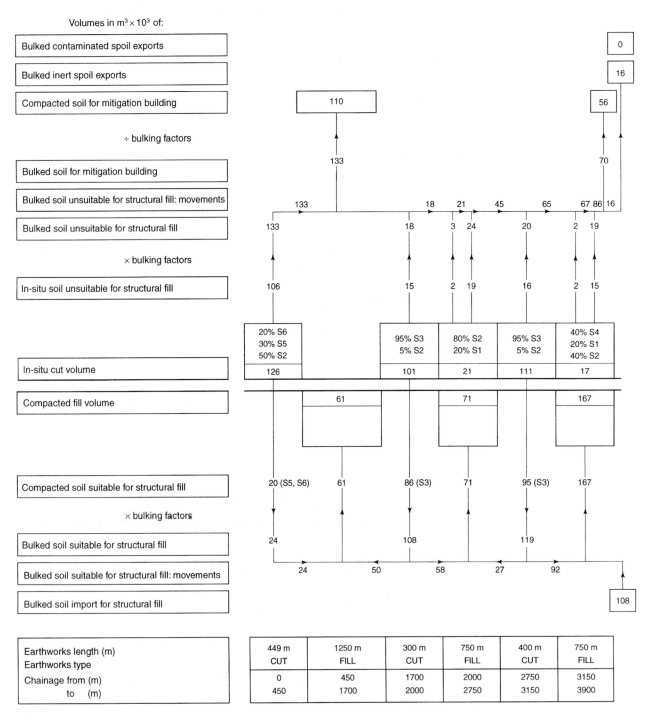

Bulked contaminated spoil exports					
Bulked inert spoil exports					
Compacted soil for mitigation building					

÷ bulking factors

Bulked soil for mitigation building					
Bulked soil unsuitable for structural fill: movements					
Bulked soil unsuitable for structural fill					

× bulking factors

| In-situ soil unsuitable for structural fill | | | | | |

| In-situ cut volume | | | | | |

| Compacted fill volume | | | | | |

| Compacted soil suitable for structural fill | | | | | |

× bulking factors

Bulked soil suitable for structural fill					
Bulked soil suitable for structural fill: movements					
Bulked soil import for structural fill					

| Earthworks length (m) Earthworks type Chainage from (m) to (m) | 449 m CUT 0 450 | 1250 m FILL 450 1700 | 300 m CUT 1700 2000 | 750 m FILL 2000 2750 | 400 m CUT 2750 3150 | 750 m FILL 3150 3900 |

Key

S1 Made ground
S2 Head
S3 Sand
S4 High plasticity overconsolidated clay
S5 Sands, silts and clays
S6 Calcareous sandstones

Figure 5.18 Earthworks movement diagram

Table 5.16 Summary of disposal, reuse and recycling of spoil anticipated at the preliminary design stage

	In-situ volume (× 1000 m³)	Bulked volume (× 1000 m³)	Compacted volume (× 1000 m³)
CUT			
Total volume of spoil generated	1616	2028	1800
Volume of spoil which is suitable as structural fill			305
Volume of spoil which is suitable as mitigation fill			1008
Volume of inert spoil which will be disposed off site		382	
Volume of contaminated spoil which will be disposed off site		55	
FILL			
Total volume of spoil needed to construct structural embankments			904
Total volume of spoil needed to construct mitigation bunding			942
BALANCE			
Deficits of spoil suitable to be reused in structural fill			599
Surplus of spoil suitable to be reused in mitigation fills			66

The Designer also identified the following alternative reuse options for the spoil from the project, as follows:

- reclamation of derelict and despoiled land
- backfilling borrow pits and disused quarries
- areas of agricultural improvement
- creation and enhancement of development land in the local area
- sale of surplus minerals (e.g. sands and gravels) to the local construction industry.

A number of local landfill sites have been identified which have sufficient capacity and which can accept the surplus spoil at its envisaged rate of generation. Particular attention is being given to the haulage routes used to transport the spoil off site to these landfills in order to minimise the environmental impact during construction.

Methods of reducing the deficit of spoil needed for structural fill are being examined. These include:

- to open up a borrow pit for Stratum 3 (Sands) to generate suitable material for the construction of the 'structural' embankments. Such a pit could be backfilled with unacceptable spoil, thus reducing the volume needing to be taken off site to landfills.
- to use slightly lower quality materials for certain fills (e.g. accommodation works)
- to use less steep side-slopes in the major cuttings through Stratum 3 (Sands)
- to replace one of the large embankments with a bridge
- to improve the foundations of one of the embankments using vibro-replacement (stone columns) or other ground treatment system, thus avoiding the need for 'dig out' of soft unacceptable material.

5.6.9 Lessons from the case study for the minimisation, reuse, recycling and disposal of excavated materials

This example shows how spoil management can be incorporated into the design of the permanent works so as to reduce the amount of material sent off site to landfill. There are number of vital components in this process, which are:

1. Carrying out a detailed desk study and comprehensive site investigation to identify which strata are suitable for use in the earthworks and to enable the excavated quantities of such strata to be estimated.

2. Understanding the cut-and-fill balance in relation to the bulk earthworks and to the different strata.

3. Early consideration of the suitability of the spoil for various uses.

4. Exploration of locations for borrow pits close to the route which could be used as inexpensive sources for earthworks construction materials and thus also create destinations for spoil unacceptable for reuse.

5. When possible, temporary and permanent works should be designed to take into account:

    *   maximum reuse of spoil

    *   the physical, geological and chemical properties of the spoil.

6 Conclusions and recommendations

6.1 GOOD PRACTICES OF SPOIL MANAGEMENT

The reviews, questionnaire survey and case studies bring to light a number of lessons for the management of spoil. It is convenient to deal with these under the heads of the planning, design and construction stages.

6.1.1 Stage 1: Project formulation

There is considerable opportunity for the Client to reduce waste disposal costs where ground engineering is a significant part of the development. If surplus material is identified at this stage, consideration should be given to relocating the material on-site and including this within the design. The Client may have environmental policies that require the promotion of environmentally sensitive approaches to project implementation. To this end credits might be given for tenders offering waste minimisation or particular initiatives that support the Client's environmental policy or ambitions. Discussion with the regulatory bodies at an early stage is important. Figure 6.1 represents choices in the planning and design stages.

Planning stage

In the planning stage, the client and designer ought to give due consideration to:

1. Recognition of the potential need for or benefit from considering options of reduction, reuse and recycling of spoil, particularly in terms of financial and environmental implications.

2. Understanding the regulatory framework and how it is being applied, particularly in relation to the classification of spoil as waste. This understanding should be developed through dialogue about the project and the nature of its surplus spoil with the Environment Agency

3. Appreciation of time-scale required for consultation and application of consents.

4. The inclusion in the desk study of the potential for off-site disposal

5. The recognition that matters such as planning and land-take affect the range of options for detailed design.

6. The advantages of early consultation with landowners.

In the case studies reviewed where a suitable landfill facility was not readily available, or the cost involved in sending spoil to landfill was high, clients have considered setting up or purchasing a landfill.

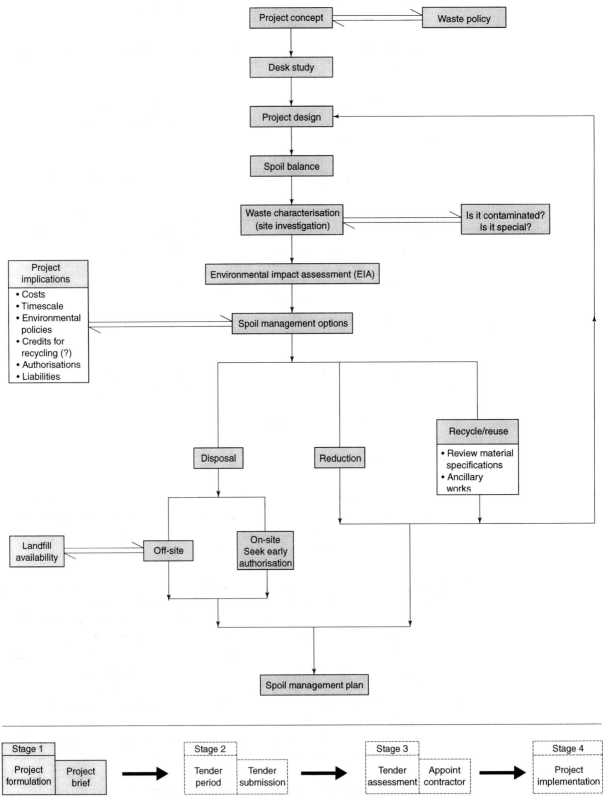

Figure 6.1   Project considerations – Stage 1: project formulation

Design stage

The design stage is critical. The assumptions then incorporated into the drawings and specification, whether about the usability of the spoil, the balance that could be achieved between cut and fill, and the freedom of landscaping (e.g. in elevation ranges) can open or reduce options for the contractor and, hence, greatly affect the cost to the client. If design for spoil management or the concept of surplus spoil reduction is not in the design brief, the consequences can be that:

1. Disposal, reuse and recycling of spoil and minimising spoil waste is unlikely to be fully integrated into project.

2. Contractors who are appointed after the project has been designed will have less control over the nature, quantity and quality of spoil that will be generated. However, they often are the sole decision-maker when choosing the disposal, reuse and recycling options for these materials.

3. There will be inadequate or inefficient communication about the management of the spoil between designer and client; designer and resident engineer; resident engineer and contractors; or of any of these with the regulator.

4. There will be confusion in the classification of waste. Case study 1 (Section 5.1) shows classification of wastes by criteria that were not necessarily indicators of contamination, but of a naturally present material. This is a question that should not just be asked at the investigation stage, but insofar as it is possible to do so, resolved with the waste regulators, so that the project costs can be maintained within the originally allowed budget.

5. Poor cut-and-fill balance will lead to the high cost of disposal or imported material or both.

If not established in the planning stage, a process of consulting the regulatory authorities should be initiated as soon as possible and maintained throughout the design stage.

6.1.2   Stages 2 and 3: Tender period and assessment

Stage 2: tender period

Waste disposal costs are an increasingly significant element within many projects involving ground engineering. All tenderers will look carefully at means of reducing waste arisings or seeking alternative uses prior to identifying disposal routes for those residual wastes that may unavoidably require disposal. Figure 6.2 represents choices in the tender period.

The nature of the material to be excavated, and its potential usefulness elsewhere, should be a major consideration. Whether the site is contaminated could have a fundamental consequence for how on-site materials would be treated and how landfill tax might apply. If potential reduction, reuse or alternative uses have been exhausted, the possible disposal of excess materials, either on-site or to adjoining land, could be the favoured option; this would need to be appraised with the regulatory authorities. Available disposal facilities within the site's perceived catchment would need to be appraised if off-site disposal is likely to be the preferred option. Whether sites are able to accept the nature of the waste in the anticipated quantities or rates can be significant constraining factors. For large projects several sites may have to be involved. This could be the case with large volumes of inert spoil as many inert sites are small in comparison to domestic, commercial or industrial waste landfills. If exempt sites, i.e. those that can accept certain (usually inert) waste materials without a requirement for a waste management licence, are identified there is a requirement, as part of the contractor's duty of care, to make sure that the site is actually exempt for the class of waste generated and that the activity being carried out at the site falls within the criteria specfied in the Waste Management Licensing Regulations 1994.

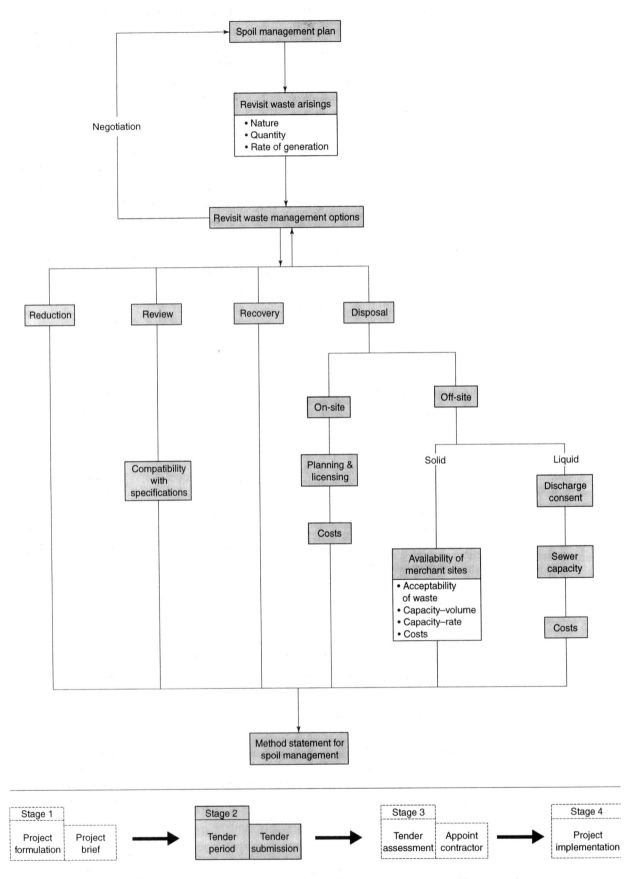

Figure 6.2 Project considerations – Stage 2: tender period (Contractor)

Stage 3 – Tender assessment

The Client will review the various management options presented by each tenderer. Cost savings are inevitably the principal criteria, but feasibility within anticipated time frame, particularly where planning and licensing consents are to be sought, could influence decision making. Any residual liability arising from on-site disposal should also be taken into account. Figure 6.3 poses questions of the client in tender assessment.

6.1.3   Stage 4: Construction

At this stage the options for realising any waste reduction are likely to be limited but should not be overlooked at the project proceeds. Planning consent and a waste management licence will be sought and hopefully secured if preceding stages have identified or resolved potential licensing or planning constraints and pitfalls. Figure 6.4 represents the implementation of the spoil management during construction.

Nevertheless there should be provision to check that the chosen reduction, reuse, and recycling and disposal options, and handling arrangements can cope with unexpected situations, e.g. if the form of the spoil is found to be more variable than had been anticipated in the design stage. Delays and extra cost can be incurred if the contractor has to change to a different landfill site, e.g. if the spoil is subsequently found to be contaminated.

Disposal of spoil off site

The questionnaire survey shows that the mid 1996 unit costs for landfilling inert spoil were between £3 and $15/m^3$ excluding landfill tax. The gate cost for contaminated spoil was on average three times more expensive.

The subject projects of the questionnaire survey and case studies (except Case Study 6 of the planning stage) are all prior to introduction of the landfill tax on 1 October 1996. During the course of the research project, however, it became clear that the tax was having a considerable effect on the management of spoil. It meant not only that greater effort was going into trying to minimise or reuse surplus spoil, but also – and perhaps counterproductive in overall environmental terms – that it had become more viable to transport surplus material greater distances.

Reuse of spoil

The potential for the reuse of spoil is often restricted by:

- the lack of suitable space on (or off) site for stockpiling
- the quantity (i.e. too much for any use, or too little for a reuse to be viable) and quality of spoil
- nature of the project, e.g. it is all in excavation.

There may be difficulties in identifying reuse options. Only a small number of the sites examined in the questionnaire survey participated in a spoil exchange scheme. Although most of the projects where surplus spoil was reused considered how to maximise reuse and to set up stockpile arrangements, none of the four projects which took part in spoil exchange had considered this at design stage.

The questionnaire survey shows that treatment of spoil was uncommon despite the fact that a quarter of sites examined generated free-draining materials or mixture of lumps, mud or slurry. Treatment would probably have been relatively expensive, when compared with the then still relatively low cost of disposal to landfill as inert waste.

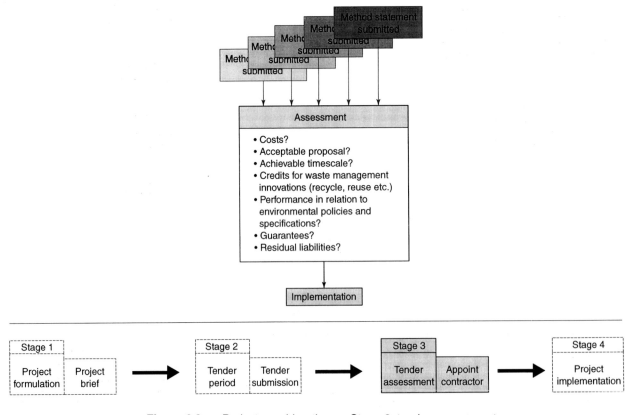

Figure 6.3   Project considerations – Stage 3: tender assessment

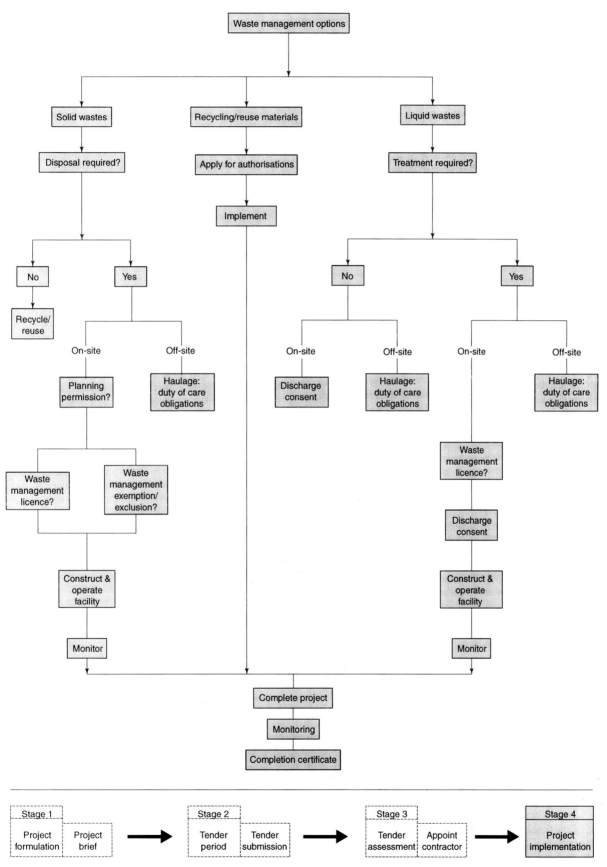

Figure 6.4   Project considerations – Stage 4: Construction (Contractor)

6.2   RECOMMENDATIONS FOR SPOIL MANAGEMENT PRACTICE

Management of spoil from ground engineering projects is a complex activity requiring careful attention at all stages of projects, particularly when the time involved in obtaining relevant permissions can be considerable and the penalties of not complying with relevant legislation are becoming increasingly severe. In addition, careful spoil management, with emphasis on waste minimisation, reuse or recovery, can bring significant financial benefits to all sides of the construction industry. In order to achieve this, all the main parties to the construction project have to improve the way they plan, design and execute the works, whichever the form of contract. Below there are lists of specific recommendations for clients, designers, contractors and, importantly, subcontractors, because so much of the work of excavating material from the ground is done by specialists. First, however, there is a recommendation for an attitude change.

Attitudes and spoil management

Waste management is not seen as an intrinsic component of construction. It is something other people do. But good engineering is about cost, and unnecessary wastage is bad management, so keeping waste to a minimum – when looked at in terms of not overdesigning a structural element, whether a concrete deck, a steel joist, a bored pile, or an embankment side slope – is seen as good engineering. So too is constructing that element efficiently, e.g. in planning the shuttering and concrete pours. The comparison of total cost in terms of efficiency is a complicated one needing a wider view than, for example, that of the reuse of the shutters. The examination of waste from ground engineering works, similarly, should not be limited to balancing, say, the need for slope stability and minimal land take. Spoil surplus increasingly now has to be brought into the reckoning.

Another aspect of attitude change stems from definitions and usage of language. The definition of what is waste is extremely complex, but once a material is called 'waste' it enters a process from which it is difficult to re-invent it as a usable or valuable commodity. It was because of the confusion created by the term 'ground engineering waste' in the title of the research project that this report refers to spoil and surplus spoil, and not to waste. In construction, 'spoil' is well understood as the winning of material from the ground. It does not prejudge what then may happen to the material. It is recommended that the terms 'spoil', 'spoil management' and 'surplus spoil' (or similar) are used for that reason, whether internally in one organisation or between different parties in the construction process. Specifically, the term should be used in consultations about the project with planners, waste regulators, and the Environment Agency. Surplus ground materials should only be referred to as wastes when their disposal as one or other category of waste is the only possible or practicable option, i.e. if there is an intention to discard.

Client

At the planning stage of the project, the Client should:
- prepare a management strategy for spoil in the planning of the project
- consult the regulatory authorities, particularly the local Environment Agency office about the reduction, reuse, recycling and disposal options considered, consents needed and identify procedures for application
- allow plenty of time for the application of planning permission and other consents needed
- include requirements on the management of spoil in the brief for the designer and in the tender documents

- allow for flexibility in alignments and level

- at the design and the construction stages of the project, insist that the design and execution of the project follows criteria set by the strategy.

Designer

The designer should advise the client that the design brief should cover the general matters listed above. In addition the designer should pay particular attention to the following:

1. Carrying out a desk study before the site investigation.

2. Incorporating within the site investigation, chemical analyses and comprehensive geotechnical testing for suitability of all earthworks and ground materials and, specifically, to test according to the classification used by the Environment Agency office.

3. Comparing the results of these analyses with the criteria in the Environment Agency's publication, *Interim Guidance in the disposal of Contaminated soils*. Thus the client and designer would not only then be aware early in the project that the spoil may be contaminated, but they would also be able to make provision for health and safety precautions in excavation, handling, transport, etc. and to evaluate different treatment options. While at the simplest level, this would allow suitable landfills to be identified more efficiently and cost-effectively, it would also form part of the necessary risk assessment under the CDM regulations.

4. Incorporating spoil management into the design stage of the project. This should involve:

   - considering the suitability of the spoil for various reuses

   - exploring opportunities such as new or already open local borrow pits that could provide a source of inexpensive fill to import to the project and create a disposal destination for the unsuitable and surplus spoil.

   - allowing flexibility in the design for spoil management

5. Considering the relaxation of earthworks specifications, so as to avoid having to reject material that is only marginally unsuitable. The option for this would have to be seen to make savings for the client without jeopardising critical quality aspects.

6. Identifying possible opportunities for reuse of surplus spoil on other projects through materials exchanges and informal networks of communication between other clients, designers, local authorities, regulators and contractors, in order to match timings as well as material types and quantities.

7. Identifying opportunities for the project to be the recipient of the surplus from other projects. This is where an ability to accept material under a different specification could provide a good cost-saving mechanism.

8. Consulting the waste regulation authority about the classification and spoil management questions that the project will pose as soon as possible and as the project develops. The earlier they are made aware of the project, the more their comment and advice can contribute to the project's success.

9. Allowing plenty of time when applying for consents.

10. Evaluating impacts of different spoil management options as part of the environmental assessment of the project.

Contractors

For a contractor, spoil management is an increasingly important component in successful tendering and profitable contract completion. A spoil management strategy could give the margin that wins a contract or improves site and project profitability.

A contractor, therefore should not just adopt techniques which make possible the reuse of spoil on or off site, but should make spoil management part of the total system of project management. Some specific matters are:

- making sure that that the Client and the Engineer understand the financial and environmental implications of the nature, degree of contamination, form and quantity of the spoil

- when formulating a plan of spoil management to prepare contingency plans to cope with variations in the nature of the spoil

- allowing good time when applying for consents.

The method statements prepared by contractors should include proposals for spoil management, in particular for that of any surplus, and should show how they will minimise the wastage of spoil and, wherever possible, adopt techniques to reuse or recycle the spoil.

6.3   CONCLUDING REMARKS

This report was written in a time of changing legislation, fiscal measures to promote sustainability, and of perceptions. The introduction of the landfill tax has changed attitudes throughout the construction industry and has led to changed practices of design and of site management. It has also had an effect, perhaps ephemeral, on the nature and amount of spoil taken to landfill sites. There is more still to be done to encourage waste minimisation but progress needs to be evaluated e.g. that the attitudinal changes do not lead to other inefficiencies or greater environmental costs in the long term.

A strategy of spoil management is more likely to be successful if it shows cost benefits for the client and the contractor. It is recommended that this subject should be studied again in a year or so in order to examine if and how practice has changed and to identify what benefits are realised. Ground engineering spoil that becomes waste represents the largest component of the construction and demolition waste-stream. For that reason alone it warrants further and continuing study as efforts continue to achieve its better management.

In conclusion the main lessons for effective spoil management are:

1.   Care is needed at all stages of projects, particularly as the time to obtain relevant permissions can be considerable and penalties of not complying with relevant legislation are increasingly severe.

2.   Efficient spoil management, with emphasis on minimisation, reuse or recovery, can bring significant financial benefits to both clients and contractors.

3.   Spoil management should be included from the start in the project brief.

4.   The Environment Agency and other regulatory authorities should be consulted as early as possible in the project and regularly thereafter.

References

1.   *Making Waste Work – A strategy for sustainable waste management in England and Wales,* DoE, December, 1995

2.   *This Common Inheritance, Britain's Environmental Strategy* HMSO, 1990.

3.   *Waste Minimisation and Recycling in Construction - review*
     P Guthrie and H Mallett, Special Publication 122, CIRIA, 1995.

4.   *Managing Demolition and Construction Wastes: Report of the Study on the Recycling of Demolition and Construction Wastes in the UK.*
     Howard Humphreys and Partners, HMSO, 1994.

5.   EC Directive 75/442/EEC, as amended by Directive 91/156/EEC. *Framework Directive on Waste.*

6.   EC Directive 78/319 replaced by 91/689 : *Hazardous Waste*

7.   EC Directive 80/68/EEC : *Protection of groundwater against pollution caused by certain dangerous substances*

8.   COM(91)102, as amended by COM(93)275 : *Landfilling of Waste.*

9.   EC Directive 85/337/EEC. *The assessment of the effects of certain public and private projects on the environment, as amended.*

10. Introduced under Part III of the *Environmental Protection Act 1990*

11. Introduced under Part I of the *Environmental Protection Act 1990*

12. Defined by the *Water Resource Act 1991*, Part III, Section 104 to include all surface and groundwater and tidal waters

13. DoE Circular 11/94 (19 April 1994) *Environmental Protection Act 1990 : Part II. Waste Management Licensing. The Framework Directive on Waste.*

14. Waste Management Licensing Regulations 1994

15. *Official Journal of the European Community*, Vol. 37 (L356), p14-22
     31 December 1994

16. *Official Journal of the European Community* Vol. 37, 31 December 1994

17. *Special Waste Regulations* 1996 (SI 1996, No 972), as amended

18. *Development of a national waste classification scheme - Stage 2 : A system for classifying wastes.* Consultation Draft, December 1995, DoE

19. PPG 23 *Planning and Pollution Control,* July 1994

20. Section 31, *Town and Country Planning Act 1990*

21. Section 26 of the *Planning and Compensation Act 1991* which introduces Section 54(a), of the *Town and Country Planning Act 1990*

22. Section 55(2) *Town and Country Planning Act 1990*

23. *Town and Country Planning (General Development Procedure) Order 1995*

24. Planning Policy Guidance Note PPG1 (1992). *General Policy and Principles.*

25. Article 20 *General Development Procedure Order 1995*

26. DoE Circular 1/85, *The Use of Conditions in Planning Permissions*

27. Section 106, *Town and Country Planning Act 1990*

28. Section 12, *Planning and Compensation Act 1991*

29. SI 1056, as amended.

30. Section 39(5) and (6). *Environmental Protection Act 1990.*

31. *The Licensing of Waste Facilities*
    Waste Management Paper 4, DoE, 1994

32. Section 36(9), *Environmental Protection Act 1990*

33. *Disposal of dredged material to land.* J Brooke, H Paipai, S E Magenis,
    S L Challinor, M Van Zijdervild, J Gibson and L Moore, Report 157,
    CIRIA, 1996

34. *Contaminated Land (16 August 1996) as introduced under the Landfill Tax
    (contaminated land) Order 1996 SI No 1529.* Landfill Tax Information
    Note 11/96

35. *A general guide to landfill tax,* Notice LFT1, H M Customs and Excise, 1997

36. *Reclamation of contaminated land,* Landfill Tax Information Note 1/97, H M
    Customs and Excise, 1 May 1997

37. ENDS Report 258, July 1996, p31

38. Section 34, *Environmental Protection Act 1990.*

39. Part III. *Environmental Protection Act 1990.*

40. *Water Resources Act 1991* Part III Section 104

41. *Special Wastes*
    Waste Management Paper 23, DoE, (in preparation)

42. *Landfill design, construction and operational practice*
    Waste Management Paper 26B, DoE, 1996

43. *Control of landfill Gas*
    Waste Management Paper 27, London (HMSO), 1991

44. *Waste minimisation and recycling in construction – site handbook*
    P M Guthrie, A C Woolveridge and V S Patel,
    Core Programme Funders Report FR/CP/41, CIRIA 1997

45. *Waste minimisation and recycling in construction – design handbook*
S Coventry and P M Guthrie
Core Programme Funders Report FR/CP/42, CIRIA (in press)

46. *Waste minimisation and recycling in construction – boardroom handbook*
S J Coventry, A C Woolveridge and V Patel
Core Programme Funders Report FR/CP/43, CIRIA (in press)

47. *Waste minimisation and recycling in construction – technical review*
P M Guthrie, S J Coventry and A C Woolveridge
Core Programme Funders Report FR/CP/44, CIRIA 1977

48. *Lime stabilisation*
CDF Rogers, S Glendinning and N Dixon, eds
Proc. Sem. at Loughborough University, 25 September 1996, Thomas Telford
Limited, 1996

49. British Standards Institution
BS 1924:

 Part 1: 1990. *General requirements, sampling, sample preparation and tests on materials before stabilization*
 Part 2: 1990 *Methods of test for cement stabilized and lime-stabilised material*

50. The solution to roadworks ahead, M. Sherrington,
Construction News, 3 October 1996

51. *Environmental Business Magazine,* October 1991

52. *Barriers, liners and cover systems for containment and control of land contamination* K D Privett, S C Matthews and R A Hodges, Special Publication 124, CIRIA 1996

53. Cutting Costs, H. Russell, Reinforced soil supplement, *New Civil Engineer*, March 1996

54. Channel Tunnel drives, construction and aspects of the disposal of tunnel spoil
C Pollard and K R Kershaw, In: *Proc. Conf. on Recycling of demolition wastes*, Int. Solid Waste and Public Cleaning Association, 1991

55. Van den Berg, R., Denneman,C.A.J. and Roels, J.M.
Risk assessment of contaminated soil proposals, for adjusted, toxicologically based Dutch soil clean-up criteria. In: *Contaminated Soil '93*, Kluwer, Dordrecht, pp 349-364.

56. Site investigation and material problems, Kelly, R.T. In: *Proceedings of a Conference on the Reclamation of Contaminated Land.* Society of Chemical Industry (London), 1980 pp B2/1-B2/14

57. *Remedial treatment for contaminated land Vol VII Ex-situ remedial methods for soils, sludges and sediments* CIRIA Special Publication 107, 1995

58. *Interim guidance on the disposal of contaminated soils* Environment Agency 2nd edition 1997

Appendix 1 Nature, form and types of spoil and the ground conditions of the site

Table A1.1 Types of projects surveyed, their ground engineering operations, spoil volumes and disposal

Site No.	Total volume of spoil (m³)	Ground engineering operations	Volume of spoil per operation (m³)	Landfill (%) off-site	Landfill (%) on-site	Reuse (%) off-site	Reuse (%) on-site	Cost (£) Disposal, reuse and recycling	Cost (£) Project
Road									
1	25000	Diaphragm wall	–	0	100	0	0	92250	35M
4	473300	Trench excavation	246000	73	0	27	0	4M	80M
		Open excavation	235000						
		Braced excavation	3700						
		Bored piling	97700						
		Cut and fill	54300						
		Structural fill	55000						
3	28000	Open excavation	13700	2.2	0	91.4	6.4	275000	110M
		Cut and fill	14300						
9	594000	Trench excavation Cut and fill Surcharging Foundation excavation	– – – –	2	0	0	98	742000	23.5M
10	621500	Cut and fill	621500	0.3	0.8	10	88.9	230000	38.7M
14	127000	Bored piling Cut and fill Excavation of structure	11000 101000 15000	100 83 93	0 0 0	0 17 7	0 0 0	1.3M	25M
15	1M	Open excavation Bored piling Trench excavation Slurry cut off wall Surcharging Cut and fill	– – – – – –	80	0	0	20	1.7M	80M
21	183000	Trench excavation Braced excavation Bored piling Top soil stripping Structural fill	– – – – –	95.6	0	0	4.4	1M	32M
26	1.2M	Trench excavation Open excavation Braced excavation Bored piling Top soil stripping Cut and fill Structural fill Site investigation boring	– – – – – – – –	80	0	0	20	Not provided	30M

Table A1.1 Types of projects surveyed, their ground engineering operations, spoil volumes and disposal (continued)

Site No.	Total volume of spoil (m^3)	Ground engineering operations	Volume of spoil per operation (m^3)	Landfill (%)		Reuse (%)		Cost (£)	
				off-site	on-site	off-site	on-site	Disposal, reuse and recycling	Project
31	687200	Trench excavation Braced excavation Bored piling Diaphragm wall Top soil stripping Cut and fill Site investigation boring Trial pits	16000 16000 16000 40000 48000 550000 200 1000	13	0	2.2	84.8	Not provided	50M
Site remediation project									
2	300000	Trench excavation Open excavation Slurry cut off wall Cut and fill Surcharging Reclamation fill Well boring Site investigation boring Trial pits	– – – – – – – – –	100	0	0	0	2500000	Not provided
5	14500	Bored piling Open excavation	– –	100	0	0	0	480000	1.4M
7	1400	Bored piling Cut and fill Grouting Lime piles	700 700 – –	70	0	0	30	6050	3.7M
23	210000	Slurry trench cut -off open excavation Cut and fill Grouting	– – – –	48	0	0	52	2.3M	7.5M
28	400000	Trench excavation Open excavation Diaphragm wall Cut and fill Top soil stripping Dynamic compaction Reclamation fill Site investigation boring Trial pits	– – – – – – – – –	10	0	0	90	4M	10M
22	100000	Mixed -in-place Reprofiling slopes Lime columns	– – –	0.01	0	99.99	0	Not provided	1.3M
17	100000	Cut and fill	–	24	0	0	76	662800	1.4M
32	25000	Open excavation Slurry trench cut-off Cut and fill Sheet pile wall	– – – –	100	0	0	0	0.55M	1.3M
34	3M	Open excavation	–	0	0	0	100	9M	11.5M

Table A1.1 Types of projects surveyed, their ground engineering operations, spoil volumes and disposal (continued)

Site No.	Total volume of spoil (m³)	Ground engineering operations	Volume of spoil per operation (m³)	Landfill (%)		Reuse (%)		Cost (£)	
				off-site	on-site	off-site	on-site	Disposal, reuse and recycling	Project
35	180000	Trench excavation Open excavation Diaphragm wall Slurry trench cut-off Well boring Site investigation boring Trial pits	– – – – – – –	77	0	0	33	6.6M	10.5M
Power station									
24	181550	Bored piling Cut and fill Foundation excavation Trench excavation	2150 115100 56600 7700	100 300 188 200	0 0 0 0	0 0 0 0	100 0 12 0	3.7M	250M
Quarry and landfill construction									
6	100000	Top soil stripping Cut and fill	– –	0.01	0	97.59	2.4	30000	4 M
8	22500	Trench excavation General excavation Top soil excavation Cut and fill	4000 1000 7500 10000	0	0	4.4	95.6	76075	15M
Commercial developments									
11	14000	Trench excavation Open excavation Bored piling	– – –	100	0	0	0	218000	24M
12	8000	Open excavation	8000	100	0	0	0	Not provided	10M
Waste water and water treatment plant									
13	16700	Open excavation Trench excavation	15400 1300	0	0	0	100	Not provided	17.7M
18	250000	Open excavation	250000	0	0	0	100	420000	30M
19	150000	Open excavation	150000	0	0	0	100	355800	25M
Tunnel									
20	92000	Tunnelling in soft ground	92000	30	0	70	0	2.3M	57M
30	160000	Auger piling Open excavation Diaphragm wall	11000 12000 29000	100	0	0	0	Not provided	Not provided
Dredging									
33	6000	Dredging	–	75	0	0	25	Not provided	380000
Pipeline									
16	Not provided	Trench excavation	–	0	0	0	100	Not provided	12.3M

Table A1.2 Spoil for ground engineering operations and site geology

Key:

D: large blocks, mixed size lumps,powdery or others e.g. boulders, rubble, etc. **M:** mixed material e.g. bentonite, slurry, pfa, lime, etc.

W: free draining, mixture of lumps and mud, slurry

Site No.	Total volume of spoil (m³)	Ground engineering operations	Volume of spoil per operation (m³)	Form	Nature of spoil	Ground conditions
Road						
1	25000	Diaphragm wall	–	W	Soft rock, sand and gravel	Lower chalk overlain by gravely head deposit.
4	473300	Trench excavation	4900 2700 3700 13300	D M M M	Stiff clay Soft clay Sand Gravel	Made ground overlying Thames Gravel, London Clay Lambeth Group, and Thanet Sand.
		Open excavation	78000 12000 30000 115000	D M M M	Stiff clay Soft clay Sand Gravel	
		Braced excavation	750 400 600 1950	D M M M	Stiff clay Soft clay Sand Gravel	
		Bored piling	39000 2400 7300 49000	D M M M	Stiff clay Soft clay Sand Gravel	
		Cut and fill	24000 33300	D D	Stiff clay Sand and gravel	
		Structural fill	55000	D	Sand and gravel	
3	28000	Open excavation Cut and fill	13700 14300	D W	Refuse Soft clay	Alluvial plain and river terrace. West of the site is low hills and ridges associated with Pleistocene glacial deposits and near surface occurrence of Triassic mudstones, sandstones and evaporites.
9	594000	Trench excavation Cut and fill Surcharging Foundation excavation	–	–	Mixed materials, and top soil	Consolidated alluvial materials overlying glacial clays.
10	621500	Cut and fill	10500 296000 110000 80000 9000 116000	D D W W W D	Hard material Stiff clay Soft clay Sand and gravel Mixed materials, Top soil	River gravel overlying Oxford Clay in turn overlying Kellaway Sand and Clay.

Table A1.2 Spoil for ground engineering operations and site geology

(continued)

Key:

D: large blocks, mixed size lumps,powdery or others e.g. boulders, rubble, etc.   **M:**   mixed material e.g. bentonite, slurry, pfa, lime, etc.

W: free draining, mixture of lumps and mud, slurry

Site No.	Total volume of spoil (m³)	Ground engineering operations	Volume of spoil per operation (m³)	Form	Nature of spoil	Ground conditions
14	127000	Bored piling Cut and fill Excavation of structures	11000 101000 15000	W W W	Stiff clay and soft rock Sand and gravel Mixed materials	The solid geology underlying the western 400 m of the route is a sequence of the Upper Coal Measures (mudstones, siltstones and occasional sandstones). In the central section of about 800 m are the mainly weak to moderately strong sandstones of the Sherwood Sandstone Group (Triassic), which at outcrop form an escarpment. Further east, the last 700 m of the new road are underlain by beds of the Mercia Mudstone Group, i.e. interbedded red-brown and green mudstones, siltstones and less frequent sandstones. The soils are represented by firm and stiff glacial tills and some localised thin alluvial deposits. The surface consists of made ground, typically 1.5 m thick, but nearly 4 m in places, represented by colliery and pottery spoil, building rubble and ash.
15	1M	Open excavation Bored piling Trench excavation Slurry cut off wall Surcharging Cut and fill	– – – – – –	D	Hard rock, stiff and soft clay, sand, gravel, mixed materials including concrete, ash	Soft Alluvium (clay and peat), made ground comprised of industrial waste. The site crosses a silt lagoon.
21	183000	Trench excavation Braced excavation Bored piling Top soil stripping Structural fill	– – – – –	D	Stiff clay, mixed materials, sand and gravel	Made ground over Boyne Hill Terrace gravel over London Clay and the Lambeth Group.
26	1.2M	Trench excavation Open excavation Braced excavation Bored piling Top soil stripping Cut and fill Structural fill Site investigation boring	– – – – – – – –	D	Stiff clay, soft clay sand and gravel, mixed materials, concrete	Not provided

Table A1.2 Spoil for ground engineering operations and site geology   (continued)

Key:

D: large blocks, mixed size lumps,powdery or others e.g. boulders, rubble, etc.   **M:** mixed material e.g. bentonite, slurry, pfa, lime, etc.

W: free draining, mixture of lumps and mud, slurry

Site No.	Total volume of spoil (m³)	Ground engineering operations	Volume of spoil per operation (m³)	Form	Nature of spoil	Ground conditions
31	687200	Trench excavation	16000	W	Stiff and soft clay, sand	The geological sequence has been created by glacial undercutting of the limestone hills on the course of a river and its tributaries. On the north of the site Lias clay is overlain by head materials, Fuller Earth, Inferior Oolite and Milford Sands.In the south of the site which fall within the river floodplain, the, Lias Clay is overlain with head material, recent alluvial deposits and terrace gravel.
		Braced excavation	16000	W	Stiff and soft clay, sand	
		Bored piling	16000	W	Stiff and soft clay	
		Diaphragm wall	40000	W	Stiff clay	
		Top soil stripping	48000	D	Top soil	
		Cut and fill	550000	W	Soft rock, stiff clay soft clay, sand and gravel	
		Site investigation boring	200	W	Hard rock, stiff clay, soft clay and sand	
		Trial pits	1000	W	Hard rock, stiff clay, soft clay and sand	
Site remediation project						
2	300000	Trench excavation Open excavation Slurry cut-off wall Cut and fill Surcharging Reclamation fill Well boring Site investigation boring Trial pits	– – – – – – – – –	W	Refuse	Municipal refuse, alluvial clays, fluvioglacial gravel, Mercia Mudstone.
5	14500	Bored piling Open excavation	– –	D	Soft clay, sand, gravel, mixed materials, ash	Made ground (ash and waste materials) overlying glacial tills (silty clays with sand layers) and Oxford clay.
7	1400	Bored piling Cut and fill Grouting Lime piles Embankment regrading	700 700	D D	Soft and stiff clay, gravel and ash	Clay and clay fill embankment core top with ash. The embankment site is on a top of alluvium and river gravel.
23	210000	Slurry trench cut off open excavation Cut and fill Grouting	– – – –	M	Mixed materials, old foundation	Abandoned site previously used as iron works and an old waste and gas work. Site underlain by carboniferous lower coal measures, principally Mudstone and shales with thin interbedded clay and ironstone seams.

Table A1.2 Spoil for ground engineering operations and site geology   (continued)

Key:

D: large blocks, mixed size lumps,powdery or others e.g. boulders, rubble, etc.   **M:**   mixed material e.g. bentonite, slurry, pfa, lime, etc.

W: free draining, mixture of lumps and mud, slurry

Site No.	Total volume of spoil (m³)	Ground engineering operations	Volume of spoil per operation (m³)	Form	Nature of spoil	Ground conditions
28	400000	Trench excavation Open excavation Diaphragm wall Cut and fill Top soil stripping Dynamic compaction Reclamation fill Site investigation boring Trial pits	– – – – – – – – –	D,W	Soft clay, sand, gravel, mixed materials	Alluvium and alluvial terrace gravel overlying the Culton and Radcliffe formations of the Triassic Merica Mudstone. An attenuated section of Triassic Sherwood sandstone occurs at moderate depth beneath.
17	100000	Cut and fill	–	D	Soft and stiff clay, silty sand, fine and medium gravel of ash, concrete slabs, foundation structures	Granular ashy fill, clay fill, alluvial clay, river gravel, Mercia Mudstone Group (with bed of siltstone).
32	25,000	Open excavation Slurry trench cut-off Cut and fill Sheet pile wall	– – – –	D	Ash, clinker, plastic and wire fragments, slag, concrete, brick structures and former foundations, sandy and clayey silty sand	Made ground, boulder clay, Clent Formation.
34	3 M	Open excavation	–	D	Fill materials, clay, coal	Fill materials, boulder clay, coal measures.
35	180000	Trench excavation Open excavation Diaphragm wall Slurry trench cut off Well boring Site investigation boring Trial pits	– – – – – – –	D, W	Soft clay, sand and gravel, mixed materials, made ground	Made ground (containing a range of gasworks contaminants), silty clay with peat (weak and compressible), Thames Gravel, London Clay, Woolwich Bed, Thanet Sand and chalk.
22	100000	Mix -in-place stabilisation Reprofiling slopes Lime columns	– – –	D	Stiff and soft clay, sand, gravel, mixed materials	Ballast at track level over variable ash and London Clay.
Power station project						
24	181550	Bored piling Cut and fill Foundation excavation Trench excavation	2000 150 7100 15000 93000 49000 7600 6100 1600	W W W W W W W W W	Stiff clay Sand and gravel Stiff clay Soft clay Mixed materials Stiff clay Sand and gravel Stiff clay Sand and gravel	Made ground clay contaminated by heavy metals and asbestos, overlying river gravels (in places) and Oxford Clay.

Table A1.2 Spoil for ground engineering operations and site geology (continued)

Key:

D: large blocks, mixed size lumps, powdery or others e.g. boulders, rubble, etc. **M:** mixed material e.g. bentonite, slurry, pfa, lime, etc.

W: free draining, mixture of lumps and mud, slurry

Site No.	Total volume of spoil (m³)	Ground engineering operations	Volume of spoil per operation (m³)	Form	Nature of spoil	Ground conditions
Quarry and landfill construction projects						
6	100000	Top soil stripping Cut and fill	– –	W, D	Top soil, soft rock, sand, gravel, slag, ash	Not provided.
8	22500	Trench excavation, Open excavation Top soil stripping Cut and fill Site investigation boring Trial pits	– – – – – –	D, W	Stiff clay silty clay, and gravel and mixed materials	Glacial sand, gravel and clay.
Commercial developments						
11	14000	Trench excavation Open excavation Bored piling	– – –	D	Stiff and soft clay, sand and gravel	Made ground with many existing foundations overlying in places flood plain gravel and London Clay.
12	8000	Open excavation	8000	M	Sand and gravel	Made ground underlain by Alluvium and Terrace Gravel and London Dense sand (Lambeth Group) below the London Clay.
Waste water and water treatment plant						
13	16700	Open excavation Trench excavation	12000 2500 900 1000 300	D D M D D	Stiff clay Soft clay Sand and gravel Stiff clay Soft clay	Filled ground with gravel, stiff clay materials with concrete.
18	250000	Open excavation	87500 75000 87500	W, M W, M W, M	Soft clay, Sand Sand and gravel	Top soil underlain by marine and estuarine alluvium, fluvio-glacial gravel and Wilmslow Sandstone of the Sherwood Sandstone Group of Triassic Age.
19	150000	Open excavation	75000 10000 65000	W W W	Sand Sludge Refuse	Domestic waste and sand.

Table A1.2 Spoil for ground engineering operations and site geology   (continued)

Key:

D: large blocks, mixed size lumps, powdery or others e.g. boulders, rubble, etc.   **M:** mixed material e.g. bentonite, slurry, pfa, lime, etc.

W: free draining, mixture of lumps and mud, slurry

Site No.	Total volume of spoil (m³)	Ground engineering operations	Volume of spoil per operation (m³)	Form	Nature of spoil	Ground conditions
Tunnel						
20	92000	Tunnelling in soft ground	23000 32500 23000 13500	D W W W	Stiff clay Soft clay Sand Gravel	The upper layer of the made up of Boulder Clay. This is a highly plastic, soft to firm glacial clay which in some areas was laminated resulting in sticky material. The clay also contains pockets of sand and gravel. The middle layer comprises fine to coarse granular sand. Within the sand are large lenses of soft laminated clays. The third layer is a hard glacial clay with many erratic boulders derived from igneous and strong sedimentary rocks. There are also large pockets of silts, sands and coarse granular deposits, all under a hydrostatic head of up to 40 m. The site was a tipping area for refuse, power station ash and agricultural waste.
30	160000	Auger piling Open excavation Diaphragm walling	11000 120000 29000	W W W	Sand and chalk Sand, clays Gravel, benonite	Lambeth Group, Thanet sands and Chalk.
Dredging						
33	6000	Dredging	–	W	Sandy silty fine, oily silty sand to coarse gravel, gravel and cobble size fragments of wood, metal, plastic, brick, plastic and organic materials	Sediment is 0.6-1.4 m below the water level. A number of materials are present on the sediment. These include black sandy silty fine, oily silty sand to coarse gravel, gravel and cobble size fragments of wood, metal, plastic, brick, plastic and organic materials. The canal bed is made up of firm red, brown and black silty sandy clay, angular to round, silty fine to coarse gravel.
Pipeline						
16	Not provided	Trench excavation	Not provided	Not provided	Soft rock, stiff and soft clay, and sand	Clay, shales, coal measures and sand.